TRAINING FOR PROFESSIONALS WHO WORK WITH GAYS AND LESBIANS IN EDUCATIONAL AND WORKPLACE SETTINGS

TRAINING FOR PROFESSIONALS WHO WORK WITH GAYS AND LESBIANS IN EDUCATIONAL AND WORKPLACE SETTINGS

Hilda F. Besner, Ph.D.
Clinical Psychologist
Fort Lauderdale, Florida

Charlotte I. Spungin, Ed.S.
Education Specialist
Fort Lauderdale, Florida

ACCELERATED DEVELOPMENT
A member of the Taylor & Francis Group

USA	Publishing Office:	ACCELERATED DEVELOPMENT
		A member of the Taylor & Francis Group
		1101 Vermont Avenue, NW, Suite 200
		Washington, DC 20005-3521
		Tel: (202) 289-2174
		Fax: (202) 289-3665
	Distribution Center:	ACCELERATED DEVELOPMENT
		A member of the Taylor & Francis Group
		1900 Frost Road, Suite 101
		Bristol, PA 19007-1598
		Tel: (215) 785-5800
		Fax: (215) 785-5515
UK		Taylor & Francis Ltd.
		1 Gunpowder Square
		London EC4A 3DE
		Tel: 0171 583 0490
		Fax: 0171 583 0581

TRAINING FOR PROFESSIONALS WHO WORK WITH GAYS AND LESBIANS IN EDUCATIONAL AND WORKPLACE SETTINGS

1 2 3 4 5 6 7 8 9 0   E B E B   9 8 7

This book was set in Times Roman. The editors were Cindy Long and Christine Winter. Technical development by Candise M. B. Heinlein. Cover design by Michelle Fleitz.

A CIP catalog record for this book is available from the British Library.
∞ The paper in this publication meets the requirements of the ANSI Standard Z39 48-1984 (Permanence of Paper)

Library of Congress Cataloging-in-Publication Data

Besner, Hilda F.
   Training for professionals who work with gays and lesbians in
educational and workplace settings / Hilda F. Besner, Charlotte
I. Spungin.
      p.   cm.
   Includes bibliographical references and index.
   ISBN 1-56032-566-6 (pbk. : alk. paper)
      1. Homosexuality and education—United States.   2. Homosexuality
in the workplace—United States.   3. Teachers—Training of—United
States.   4. Employee training personnel—Training of—United States.
5, Homosexuality—Study and teaching—United States.   6. Activity
programs in education—United States.   I. Spungin, Charlotte I.
II. Title
LC192.6.B49   1997   97-20520
378.1'2'0683—dc21   CIP

ISBN 1-56032-566-6 (paper)

For Mark, Adriana, Hanna,
Mom, Dad, Adele, Allyson, Jason,
Tyler, Eleanor,
and in memory of
Sharon

CONTENTS

PREFACE

Several leading national academic organizations recently have taken steps to address the needs of gay and lesbian youth by passing antidiscrimination resolutions and/or providing educational guidelines to facilitate changes in awareness, curriculum, and professional development. Among these organizations are the National Education Association, the Association for Supervision and Curriculum Development, Phi Delta Kappa, the American Counseling Association, the American Library Association, the American School Health Association, and the American Psychological Association. In addition, various political and governmental organizations, such as the American Federation of Teachers and state departments of education, also are providing leadership to influence change.

Most of the gay and lesbian students in our schools blend into the student populations and are assumed to be heterosexual by their friends, classmates, and school personnel. Those students who feel unable to declare their diverse sexual orientations pretend to be heterosexual and, in self-defense, play this role throughout their school experience.

Research has indicated that approximately one out of every ten people is gay or lesbian. Too many heterosexuals in our society erroneously believe they can identify gays and lesbians by using the stereotypes that have been passed on from one generation to another. Nothing could be further from the truth. Many young people and adults are labeled as gay or lesbian simply because they fit the gay or lesbian stereotypes when, in fact, their sexual orientation is heterosexual.

Gay and lesbian students who realize the potential danger in publicly disclosing their sexual orientation may try to hide their sexuality by dating the opposite sex and pretending to be heterosexual. This denial of sexual orientation can lead to a multitude of problems, such as suicide attempts, suicides, academic failure, dropping out of school, drug and alcohol abuse, alienation from parents and friends, running away from home, and teenage pregnancies.

The purpose of this manual is to provide a model for training of inservice college professors and instructors who prepare educators and business professionals for their professions, workplace executives and managers, school personnel, and other professionals whose occupations place them in contact with young people. The intention is to prepare these participants to replicate the training for their colleagues. This procedure of training trainers is the most effective method for providing help for thousands of gay and lesbian students who are attending secondary schools and colleges and who will eventually join the workplace.

ACKNOWLEDGMENTS

Whatever anyone accomplishes, others always help, and with this in mind, the authors would like to express their gratitude to the following people: Dr. Joseph Hollis for his vision and guidance; Cindy Long for coordinating the publication; Christine Winter for a meticulous copy-editing job; Michelle Fleitz for her creative cover design; Mark Colin for his emotional support and assistance; and Adriana and Hanna for their love, understanding, and sharing their mother with this project, all of which helped facilitate the completion of the manuscript.

Hilda Besner
Charlotte Spungin

INTRODUCTION

There are compelling reasons for addressing gay and lesbian issues in educational settings and in the workplace. As with any oppressed minority group, many gay and lesbian people experience prejudice, discrimination, and violent behavior that is usually motivated by fear, misinformation, and/or lack of knowledge; education can be a powerful instrument for change.

The dual focus on the educational and workplace settings emphasizes that recognition and acceptance of diversity can be the result of formal and continuing education.

The authors hope that after experiencing the activity modules, the educational professionals and workplace leaders will perceive the urgency for replicating the training among their colleagues and this manual will become a tool for change.

The following lists potential workshop participants in both the educational and workplace categories:

Workplace Settings	Educational Settings
Corporate executives	Inservice and preservice teachers
Middle managers	School district administrators
Human resource department personnel	School building administrators
Employees	Guidance counselors
Employee organizations	Visiting teachers
Personnel directors	School nurses
Employee assistance personnel	School psychologists
	Social workers
	Educators' organizations
	Curriculum directors

Continued

Workplace Settings	Educational Settings
	Media specialists
	Human resources development personnel
	School board members
	Undergraduate and graduate professors and instructors of education, business administration, social work, behavioral sciences, nursing, etc.

EXPERIENCE-BASED LEARNING

Learning researchers have established that experiential learning involving challenge, spontaneity, creativity, group decision-making, brainstorming, and cooperative learning results in participants' having greater retention and in-depth learning. The authors believe that experiential learning produces a high degree of transfer of learning to the educational setting or the workplace; therefore, the training activities in this manual have been developed to involve participants in group interaction as they learn, and the trainer's role is that of a facilitator.

GOALS OF THE WORKSHOP ACTIVITIES

The activities in this training manual have been designed to:

- promote an awareness and understanding of the specific needs and issues associated with students who have diverse sexual orientations;
- provide information, based on research, concerning homophobia and its effects;
- present research-based theories on the causes of homosexuality;
- introduce ways school personnel can assist gay and lesbian students with self-acceptance, building positive self-concepts, and increasing self-esteem;
- create an awareness of the necessity for preparing gay and lesbian students for the workplace;
- familiarize participants with the issue of students with gay and lesbian parents;
- acquaint participants with the literature, national organizations, and educational projects that deal with gays and lesbians in educational and workplace settings; and/or

- motivate participants to assume responsibility for presenting the inservice content to groups of their colleagues.

STRUCTURE OF AND TRAINING METHODS FOR WORKSHOP ACTIVITIES

Each workshop activity includes the following information:

- title of activity,
- objective(s) for the activity,
- estimated time needed for completion of the activity,
- list of materials needed, and
- directions for the facilitators.

In addition, many of the activities include the following, if necessary:

- background information for facilitators,
- supportive training materials (e.g., handouts, transparencies, and charts),
- directions for the participants,
- questions for discussion, and
- key points for facilitators to elicit.

The training methods used to implement the activities are as follows:

- structured exercises,
- facilitators' presentations,
- role-playing,
- group discussions,
- simulation,
- readings,
- questionnaires,
- case studies,
- inventories,
- brainstorming,
- interview,
- forced field analysis,
- problem-solving,
- action planning, and
- fishbowl.

STEPS FOR PLANNING A WORKSHOP AGENDA

1. Decide on the amount of time to be devoted to the workshop. [Deduct time for breaks, lunch, and structured exercises (e.g., icebreakers) to determine actual content time.]
2. Review the chart below. It includes the following information:
   - the sections and activities of the manual;
   - the estimated time for completion of each activity; and
   - the focus of each activity (1) generic, (2) workplace setting, or (3) educational setting.

[The timing for delivery of a workshop varies with different facilitators and groups of participants; for this reason, estimated times have been maximized.]

3. Select from the chart, sections and activities that meet the needs of the workshop participants and conform to the workshop time constraints. [Note: Certain items should be included in every workshop agenda:

   - at least two structured activities from Section I for each day of the workshop,
   - Individual Action Plans (Section X),
   - Review of Resources (Section XII), and
   - Evaluation of the Workshop (Section XIII).]

4. Read through the chosen sections and activities to make sure they meet the requirements for the specific workshop being planned.
5. Review Section XII to see if any resources need to be ordered.
6. Draft the workshop agenda.

Content	Estimated Time (min)	Focus Generic	Work-place Setting	Educa-tional Setting
Section I: Structured Activities (icebreakers, getting acquainted, energizers)				
Activity 1.1: My Expectations	20–25	x		
Activity 1.2: Participant Interviews	25–30	x		
Activity 1.3: Group Interaction	15–20	x		
Activity 1.4: Getting Acquainted	15–20	x		
Activity 1.5: Talk with a Stranger	10–15	x		

Continued

	Focus			
Content	**Estimated Time (min)**	**Generic**	**Work-place Setting**	**Educa-tional Setting**
Activity 1.6: Greatest Achievement	15–20	x		
Activity 1.7: Half-Time Review	10–15	x		
Activity 1.8: Discovery	15–20	x		
Activity 1.9: Test Your Ingenuity	15–20	x		
Section II: Self-Assessment				
Activity 2.1: Self-Exploration	10–15	x		
Activity 2.2: Developmental Aspects of Sexuality	20–30	x		
Activity 2.3: Self-Assessment Inventory	25–30	x		
Activity 2.4: Belief Statements Regarding Gays and Lesbians	25–30	x		
Section III: Origins of Homosexuality				
Activity 3.1: What Causes Homosexuality?	15–20	x		
Activity 3.2: Understanding the Origins of Homosexuality	30–45	x		
Activity 3.3: Facts about Homosexuality	55–60	x		
Activity 3.4: Famous Gays and Lesbians	20–25	x		
Section IV: Homophobia				
Activity 4.1: Homophobia: Significant Historical Events	15–20	x		
Activity 4.2: Motivations for Homophobic Thought and Behavior	35–40	x		
Activity 4.3: Fact or Myth?	40–50	x		
Activity 4.4: Types of Homophobia	25–30	x		
Activity 4.5: The Impact of Homophobia on Gay and Lesbian Youth	20–25			x
Activity 4.6: Effects of Homophobia Experienced by Gay and Lesbian Students	45–50			x
Activity 4.7: Readings and Discussion	25–30			x
Activity 4.8: Educating to Reduce and Prevent Homophobia	45–50	x		

Table *Continued*

	Focus			
Content	**Estimated Time (min)**	**Generic**	**Work- place Setting**	**Educa- tional Setting**
Activity 4.9: Beliefs Concerning Gays and Lesbians	30–40	x		
Activity 4.10: Consequences of Actions Relative to Gays and Lesbians	55–60	x		
Section V: Identifying and Assisting Youth in Need				
Activity 5.1: Brainstorming At-Risk Behavioral Indicators	40–45			x
Activity 5.2: Case Study: Aaron Fricke	35–40			x
Activity 5.3: Providing Assistance for Youth with Diverse Sexual Orientations	40–45			x
Section VI: Educational and Workplace Issues and Programs to Promote Positive Change				
Activity 6.1: Identifying Issues in the Workplace	55–60		x	
Activity 6.2: Case Studies: Jane Doe, Joyce, Jim, and Mr. Russell	55–60		x	x
Activity 6.3: What Would You Do?	25–30		x	x
Activity 6.4: Problems and Solutions Associated with Gays and Lesbians in Educational and Workplace Settings	40–45		x	x
Activity 6.5: Promoting Positive Attitudes at School and in the Workplace	80–90		x	x
Section VII: Closeted Gays and Lesbians				
Activity 7.1: Speculations Regarding the Lives of Closeted Gays/Lesbians	45–50	x		
Activity 7.2: Interview: Senior Citizens in Retrospect	30–35	x		
Activity 7.3: Special Problems of the Gay and Lesbian Elderly	20–30	x		
Activity 7.4: Case Study: Karen	40–50	x		

Table   *Continued*

USE OF VIDEOTAPES

The videotapes listed in Section XII may be used to support a workshop agenda. They offer realism, reinforce concepts, provide a high-impact and interesting learning experience, and can vary the pace of the workshop day. Most facilitators are aware of the fact that videotapes are a uniquely flexible and versatile tool; they can be used to introduce a workshop topic, to reinforce a topic already presented, or to help summarize a workshop.

Previewing a videotape helps facilitators decide how it will be used to enhance the workshop agenda (e.g., a decision may be made to show pertinent segments rather than one entire videotape). During the preview session, take notes regarding the following:

- the issues the video raises,
- the issues the video answers, and
- the significant events or situations that should be emphasized.

Introduce the videotape to participants by using an opening statement that will challenge and motivate them. Tell them what to look for as they view the tape, and defuse possible negative reactions by letting them know they may see or hear something they may not like or with which they may not agree.

Post-videotape activities will depend on individual facilitators and the composition of the participants, but the following general questions may be addressed through the use of small groups (dyads, triads, etc.):

- What lessons can be learned from the content of the videotape?
- With what did you disagree? agree?
- What are the implications of the videotape for the workplace/educational setting?

The following chart lists the videotapes from Section XII, the estimated running time, and suggestions for their appropriate usage. This chart will assist facilitators with their workshop plans. Videotape ordering information and descriptions are located in Section XII.

Title of Videotape	Time	Suggested Use
A Little Respect	25 min	Section IV
Another Side of the Closet	30 min	Section IX
Be True to Yourself	28 min	Section V
Before Stonewall	87 min	Sections IV, VII

Continued

Title of Videotape	Time	Suggested Use
Both of My Moms' Names Are Judy	10 min	Section IX
Families Come Out	30 min	Section IX
Gay Issues in the Workplace	25 min	Sections VI, VIII
Gay Youth	40 min	Section V
Homosexuality: The Adolescent's Perspective	30 min	Section V
Not All Parents Are Straight	58 min	Section IX
On Being Gay (2 parts)	80 min	Sections III, V
Pink Triangles: A Study of Prejudice Against Lesbians and Gay Men	35 min	Section IV
Reunion: One Family Overcomes Religious Homophobia	30 min	Section IV
Running Gay	20 min	Sections III, VIII
Sexual Orientation: Reading Between the Labels	30 min	Section V
Sticks, Stones, and Stereotypes (Spanish and English versions)	20 min	Section IV
Teens Speak Out	45 min	Section V
What If I'm Gay? A Search for Understanding	29- and 47-min versions	Sections III, V
Who's Afraid of Project 10?	23 min	Sections V, VI

USE OF AUDIOTAPES

The creative use of audiotapes can have a positive effect on participants' learning. All but one of the audiotapes listed in Section XII were professionally recorded at the 1995 national convention of Parents, Families and Friends of Lesbians and Gays (P-FLAG). Preview of these tapes and the selection of 5- or 10-minute segments to be appropriately integrated throughout a workshop can enhance participants' learning. For example, hearing the testimonials of gays, lesbians, and their parents is a thought-provoking experience and can have significant positive effects on feelings and attitudes. Unlike videotapes, audiotapes require an active imagination to create images, and this active participation can result in a uniquely meaningful experience for learners.

The Following chart lists the audiotape titles from Section XII and their suggested uses. (See Section XII for ordering information.)

Title of Audiotape	Suggested Use
Accepting Your Gay or Lesbian Child (Parents Share Their Stories)	Section V
Reaching Out to and Educating Community/Corporate Leaders	Section VI

Continued

Title of Audiotape	Suggested Use
Opening Corporate America to P-FLAG	Section VI
The Challenges and Opportunities in 1996 for Gay, Lesbian,	
Bisexual and Transgendered Youth	Section V
Gays and Lesbians in the Workplace Environment	Section VI
Teens Tell Their Own Stories	Section IV, V
So Just What Does a School Board Do?	Sections VI, X

SAMPLE WORKSHOP AGENDAS

Although the training materials are designed for a two/three-day workshop, they can be adapted easily to specific time allotments through manipulation of the activities. Facilitators for the training should be experienced in presenting inservice programs to professionals, because they will be modeling training skills for the participants who will be replicating the training for their colleagues. Below are several sample agendas to assist in planning a workshop.

Three-Day Workshop
Participants: 10 to 25 Secondary School Principals

Day 1
Registration
Welcoming Remarks (Facilitator)
Section I: Structured Activities
    Activity 1.1: My Expectations
Section II: Self-Assessment
    Activity 2.1: Self-Exploration
    Activity 2.2: Developmental Aspects of Sexuality
    Activity 2.3: Self-Assessment Inventory
    Activity 2.4: Belief Statements Regarding Gays and Lesbians

Break

Section III: Origins of Homosexuality
    Activity 3.1: What Causes Homosexuality
    Activity 3.2: Understanding the Origins of Homosexuality
    Activity 3.3: Facts about Homosexuality
    Activity 3.4: Famous Gays and Lesbians

Lunch

Section I: Structured Activities
    Activity 1.7: Half-Time Review

Section IV: Homophobia
   Activity 4.1: Homophobia: Significant Historical Events
   Activity 4.2: Motivations for Homophobic Thought and Behavior
   Activity 4.6: Effects of Homophobia Experienced
      by Gay and Lesbian Students
   Activity 4.8: Educating to Reduce and Prevent Homophobia
Adjournment

Day 2
Registration
Welcoming Remarks (Facilitators)
Section I: Structured Activities
   Activity 1.9: Test Your Ingenuity
Section V: Identifying and Assisting Youth in Need
   Activity 5.1: Brainstorming At-Risk Behavioral Indicators
   Activity 5.2: Case Study: Aaron Fricke

Break

   Activity 5.3: Providing Assistance for Youth with Diverse Sexual Orientations
Section I: Structured Activities
   Activity 1.7: Half-Time Review

Lunch

Section I: Structured Activities
   Activity 1.6: Greatest Achievement
Section VI: Educational and Workplace Issues and Programs
   to Promote Positive Change
   Activity 6.2: Case Study: Mr. Russell [Handout 6.2 (Part D)]
   Activity 6.5: Promoting Positive Attitudes at School
      and in the Workplace

Break

Section VIII: Preparing Gay and Lesbian Students for the Workplace
   Activity 8.1: Nurturing Self-Esteem and Communicating the Existence
      of a Safe Environment
   Activity 8.3: Gay-Friendly Companies
Adjournment

Day 3
Registration
Welcoming Remarks (Facilitators)
Section I: Structured Activities
   Activity 1.8: Discovery

Section I: Structured Activities
  Activity 1.8: Discovery
Section III: Origins of Homosexuality
  Activity 3.4: Famous Gays and Lesbians
Section I: Structured Activities
  Activity 1.7: Half-Time Review

Lunch

Section IV: Homophobia
  Activity 4.1: Homophobia: Significant Historical Events
  Activity 4.3: Fact or Myth?
  Activity 4.4: Types of Homophobia
  Activity 4.5: The Impact of Homophobia on Gay and Lesbian Youth

Break

Section IV: Homophobia
  Activity 4.6: Effects of Homophobia Experienced by Gay
    and Lesbian Students
Videotape: *Gay Youth*
Adjournment

Day 2
Registration
Welcoming Remarks (Facilitators)
Section IV: Homophobia
  Activity 4.7: Readings and Discussion
  Activity 4.8: Educating to Reduce and Prevent Homophobia
Section I: Structured Activities
  Activity 1.9: Test Your Ingenuity

Break

Section V: Identifying and Assisting Youth in Need
  Activity 5.1: Brainstorming At-Risk Behavioral Indicators
  Activity 5.3: Providing Assistance for Youth with Diverse Sexual Orientations
Videotape: *Teens Speak Out* (selected segments)
Section I: Structured Activities
  Activity 1.7: Half-Time Review

Lunch

Section VII: Closeted Gays and Lesbians
  Activity 7.2: Interview: Senior Citizens in Retrospect

Section VIII: Preparing Gay and Lesbian Students for the Workplace
   Activity 8.1: Nurturing Self-Esteem and Communicating
   the Existence of a Safe Environment
Adjournment

Day 3
Registration
Welcoming Remarks (Facilitators)
Section I: Structured Activities
   Activity 1.6: Greatest Achievement
Section VIII: Preparing Gay and Lesbian Students for the Workplace
   Activity 8.2: Workshop to Prepare Gay and Lesbian Students for the
   Workplace

Break

Section VIII: Preparing Gay and Lesbian Students for the Workplace
   Activity 8.3: Gay-Friendly Companies
Section IX: Students with Gay or Lesbian Parents
   Activity 9.1: Statistics Related to Gay and Lesbian Parents
   Activity 9.2: Gay and Lesbian Parental Issues
   Activity 9.3: Parents' Sexuality and Its Impact on Children

Lunch

Section IX: Students with Gay or Lesbian Parents
   Activity 9.4: Educators Working with Gay and Lesbian Parents
Videotape: *Not All Parents Are Straight*
Section X: Individual Action Plans
   Activity 10.2: Development of Participants'
   Individual Action Plans
Section XII: Review of Resources
Section XIII: Evaluation of the Workshop
   Activity 13.1: Evaluation of the Workshop
Adjournment

Two-Day Workshop
Participants: 10 to 20 Corporate Executives

Day 1
Registration
Welcoming Remarks (Facilitators)
Section I: Structured Activities

Activity 1.1: My Expectations
Activity 1.3: Group Interaction
Section II: Self-Assessment
    Activity 2.1: Self-Exploration
    Activity 2.2: Developmental Aspects of Sexuality
    Activity 2.3: Self-Assessment Inventory

Break

Section III: Origins of Homosexuality
    Activity 3.2: Understanding the Origins of Homosexuality
    Activity 3.3: Facts about Homosexuality
    Activity 3.4: Famous Gays and Lesbians
Section I: Structured Activities
    Activity 1.7: Half-Time Review

Lunch

Section IV: Homophobia
    Activity 4.1: Homophobia: Significant Historical Events
    Activity 4.2: Motivations for Homophobic Thought and Behavior
    Activity 4.3: Fact or Myth?
Videotape: *Pink Triangles: A Study of Prejudice Against Lesbian and Gay Men*
Section IV: Homophobia
    Activity 4.9: Beliefs Concerning Gays and Lesbians
Adjournment

Day 2
Registration
Welcoming Remarks (facilitators)
Section VI: Educational and Workplace Issues and Programs
    to Promote Positive Change
        Activity 6.4: Problems and Solutions Associated with Gays
        and Lesbians in Educational and Workplace Settings
        (use workplace handout only)
        Activity 6.2: Case Studies: Jane Doe, Joyce, and Jim
        [Handout 6.2 (Parts A, B, & C)]
Break
Videotape: *Gay Issues in the Workplace*
Section VI: Educational and Workplace Issues and Programs
    to Promote Positive Change
        Activity 6.5: Promoting Attitudes at School and in the Workplace
        [Handout 6.5 (Part A)]

STRUCTURED ACTIVITIES

The purpose of this section is to provide facilitators with several structured activities to help participants get acquainted, build trust, and become energized during the training. Selection of activities and determining when to use them will be decided by the facilitators. These decisions will be influenced by such factors as how well participants already know one another, time constraints, and the design of individual workshops. Usually, training sessions are most successful when some time is devoted to structured activities that are nonthreatening and unrelated to the content of the workshop.

The following chart is provided to assist facilitators with selection and scheduling of the structured activities.

Title of Structured Activity	Activity Objective(s)	Best Purpose/ Time to Use During Workshop	Estimated Time for Completion of Activity
1.1. My Expectations	To focus participants' attention on the training program To develop ground rules for the workshop To alert participants to expect group interaction	Beginning of workshop	20–25 min
1.2. Participant Interviews	To help participants get acquainted with each other	Early on during workshop	25–30 min

Continued

1

Title of Structured Activity	Activity Objective(s)	Best Purpose/ Time to Use During Workshop	Estimated Time for Completion of Activity
1.3. Group Interaction	To establish readiness for participants to work through the sharing of personal experiences	Icebreaker Early on during workshop	15–20 min
1.4. Getting Acquainted	To involve participants in communicating about themselves	Early on during workshop	15–20 min
1.5. Talk with a Stranger	To involve participants in communicating about themselves	Getting acquainted with participants Anytime during workshop	10–15 min
1.6. Greatest Achievement	To establish the process of sharing personal information	Icebreaker Early on during workshop	15–20 min
1.7. Half-Time Review	To review important points and/or generalizations acquired during the first half of the workshop To have participants compare their perceptions of the workshop content	Halfway through the workshop agenda	10–15 min
1.8. Discovery	To help participants get acquainted with each other	Early on during workshop	15–20 min
1.9. Test Your Ingenuity	To stress the importance of collaboration, pooling of different perceptions, and creative thinking in problem-solving	Energizer Anytime during workshop	15–20 min

Activity 1.1
MY EXPECTATIONS

Objectives: To focus participants' attention on the training program; to develop ground rules for the workshop; to alert participants to expect group interaction, rather than passive attendance

Estimated Time: Approximately 20 to 25 minutes

Materials Needed: Handout 1.1: My Expectations (one copy for each participant)

Directions for Facilitators

1. Organize participants into groups of six.
2. Distribute copies of Handout 1.1 to all participants and ask them to complete the form.
3. After forms have been completed, collect them and read aloud several responses in each category listed on the form.
4. Initiate a discussion of the participants' expectations and focus on the objectives for the activity. [Be sure to include the following: Success of the workshop will depend on the willingness of participants: (a) to take an active part in the workshop activities, (b) to share ideas, (c) to actively listen to others, (d) to be open to new ideas, and (e) to respect the opinions and ideas of others.]

Handout 1.1
MY EXPECTATIONS

Directions for Participants

1. Please write your response to each of the following.
2. You need not write your name on the sheet.
3. When you have finished, please give the sheet to the group facilitator, who will share your comments with others.

What I expect from facilitators:

_____

_____

_____

What I expect from the other participants:

_____

_____

_____

What I expect from myself as a participant:

_____

_____

_____

What I expect to learn during the workshop:

_____

_____

_____

Handout 1.1. Permission is granted to photocopy for classroom use.

Activity 1.2
PARTICIPANT INTERVIEWS

Objective: To help participants get acquainted with each other
Estimated Time: 25 to 30 minutes
Materials Needed: Handout 1.2: Get Acquainted Sheet (one copy for each participant)

Directions for Facilitators

1. Organize participants into groups of six. (Work in dyads within each group.)
2. Distribute Handout 1.2 to each participant.
3. Ask both people in each dyad to interview one another and complete the information on the Get Acquainted Sheet(s), Handout 1.2.
4. When everyone has finished interviewing (about 10 minutes), ask each person to introduce the person interviewed to the entire group of participants by reading the interviewee's responses to the 11 items on the Get Acquainted Sheet.
5. Collect the sheets to keep as background information on each participant.

Handout 1.2
GET ACQUAINTED SHEET

Directions for Participants

1. Interview a member of the group and write his or her response to each of the following 11 items.
2. When instructed to do so, read for benefit of the group the interviewee's response.
3. Submit the completed sheet to the facilitator.

1. Name of person interviewed:

_____

_____

2. Job description (position, name of workplace):

_____

_____

3. Hobby:

_____

_____

4. Hometown and state:

_____

_____

5. High school/college/university attended:

_____

_____

6. Favorite TV program:

_____

_____

7. Favorite type of music:

_____

_____

8. Favorite food:

_____

_____

9. Favorite sports team:

_____

_____

10. One thing that really bugs him/her:

_____

_____

11. If he/she won a million dollar lottery, he/she would:

_____

_____

Handout 1.2.   Permission is granted to photocopy for classroom use.

Activity 1.3
GROUP INTERACTION

Objective: To establish readiness for participants to work together through the sharing of personal experiences

Estimated Time: Approximately 15 to 20 minutes

Materials Needed: Handout 1.3: Conversation Stems Sheet (one copy for each group)

Directions for Facilitators

1. Organize participants into groups of four or six.
2. Distribute one copy of Handout 1.3 to each subgroup and direct them as follows: "Pass the Conversation Stems Sheet around the group and each person select a stem he or she wishes to talk about. Each person in the group should have a turn to speak to the group regarding his or her selected stem. The focus should be on personal experiences and feelings. The 'listeners' may make comments."
3. Circulate and tactfully intervene if one person is dominating a group.
4. End the small group discussions after 15 or 20 minutes.
5. Initiate a brief discussion regarding the members' comfort level with the small group discussions.

Handout 1.3
CONVERSATION STEMS SHEET

Directions for Participants

1. Each person in your group is to select one of the following 20 stem sentences to complete.
2. Prepare yourself to talk to the group using your chosen stem sentence.

1.   When it comes to lesbians and gay men, I . . .
2.   When I see an article in a newspaper or magazine about legalizing gay and lesbian marriage, I . . .
3.   The teacher who meant the most to me was a person who . . .
4.   When it comes to derogatory jokes about gays or lesbians, I . . .
5.   Personal success is marked by . . .
6.   Unconditional love is . . .
7.   One thing I hate is . . .
8.   My coworkers think of me as . . .
9.   One thing I like about myself is . . .
10. When I see a gay man or lesbian woman on a TV talk show, I . . .
11. An experience in school that really upset me was . . .
12. I am most effective in my job when . . .
13. A recent movie I really liked was . . .
14. Computers . . .
15. One time in my life when I spoke my mind was . . .
16. I would like to be . . .
17. Gay bashers . . .
18. Sometimes I feel . . .
19. The main thing that frustrates me at work is . . .
20. When I found out a friend of mine was gay/lesbian, I . . .

Activity 1.4
GETTING ACQUAINTED

Objective: To involve participants in communicating about themselves
Estimated Time: 15 to 20 minutes
Materials Needed: None

Directions for Facilitators

1. Organize participants into groups of six.
2. Ask participants in each group to select three items from their wallets and tell the other members of the group why each item is important to their lives. (Examples: a membership card, a bookstore discount card, a business card, a photograph)

Activity 1.5
TALK WITH A STRANGER

Objective: To involve participants in communicating about themselves
Estimated Time: 10 to 15 minutes
Materials Needed: None

Directions for Facilitators

1. Explain to the group of workshop participants that they will be working together for the duration of the workshop and they should try to get to know one another on more than a superficial basis.
2. Ask participants to circulate around the room and find a person they do not know very well. Tell them to introduce themselves and talk with their partners for about 5 minutes. They may talk about anything, but it is preferable to talk about themselves (e.g., educational background, places traveled, most embarrassing experience in elementary school, first job experience, favorite subject in high school/college, hobbies, previous jobs as an adult, fraternity/sorority memberships, talents, etc.).
3. Remind participants to give both partners equal time to talk during the allotted time frame.
4. Initiate discussion with the questions provided.

Questions for Discussion

1. Why don't we always take the time to talk with our colleagues in the workplace?
2. What are the advantages of talking with our colleagues about their uniqueness?
3. What would you reveal about yourself to a colleague you knew only superficially?

Activity 1.6
GREATEST ACHIEVEMENT

Objective: To establish the process of sharing personal information
Estimated Time: 15 to 20 minutes
Materials Needed: None

Directions for Facilitators

1. Organize participants into groups of four or six.
2. Ask participants to take a moment to think of their greatest achievement. Tell them they will have less than a minute to share it with their small group.
3. After a moment of "think time," begin the round of sharing by disclosing your own greatest achievement and why. Then ask participants to share within their small groups.
4. Initiate a large group discussion using the questions provided.

Questions for Discussion

1. Of what value is the exercise for the participants of this workshop?
2. Of what value is nonthreatening disclosure of personal information?

Activity 1.7
HALF-TIME REVIEW

Objectives: To review important points and/or generalizations acquired during the first half of the workshop; to have participants compare their perceptions of the workshop content
Estimated Time: 10 to 15 minutes
Materials Needed: Flip chart, easel, and markers for facilitators; paper and pens or pencils for participants

Directions for Facilitators

1. Organize participants into groups of four or six.
2. Just before lunch or a scheduled break, remind the participants that a number of major points have been covered during the first half of the workshop and it is time for a quick review.
3. Ask participants to write at least six major ideas or key points they have learned, or conclusions they have drawn, regarding the first half of the workshop content.
4. When most participants seem to be finished writing, ask for responses from various participants and list them on the flip chart until at least 10 or 12 are listed. Then ask participants to compare their lists with the list of one other person in their subgroups, to determine similarities and dissimilarities.
5. Initiate discussion using the questions provided.

Questions for Discussion

1. How was your list different from the list of others in your group?
2. Is there any value in learning what others thought were important points in the workshop content?

Activity 1.8
DISCOVERY

Objective: To help participants get acquainted with each other
Estimated Time: 15 to 20 minutes
Materials Needed: Handout 1.8: Discovery List (one copy for each participant); pencils for all participants

Directions for Facilitators

1. Tell participants this activity is being used to help them get acquainted and learn something special about other participants.
2. Distribute one copy of Handout 1.8 to each participant.
3. Ask them to circulate around the room and interview people, with the objective of finding one different individual who qualifies for each statement on the Discovery List. Remind them that the same person cannot be listed for more than one statement. Ask them to write in the person's name and job description.
4. After about 15 minutes, ask everyone to take a seat. Stimulate discussion using the questions provided.

Questions for Discussion

1. What were some interesting things you discovered from doing this activity?
2. Did anyone discover some things in common with the participants interviewed?
3. How many of you finished the activity during the allotted time frame? Why didn't some of you finish the list?

Handout 1.8
DISCOVERY LIST

Directions for Participants

1. Please identify fellow group members who fit any of the following 10 descriptions.
2. Circulate around the room and find different individuals for each of the statements that follow.
3. Fill in each person's name and job description. (A person's name may NOT appear more than once.)
4. You will have 15 minutes to complete this activity.

1. Discover a person who plays a musical instrument.
   Name: _____
   Job description: _____

2. Discover a person who has served in the military.
   Name: _____
   Job description: _____

3. Discover a person who was a Boy Scout or a Girl Scout.
   Name: _____
   Job description: _____

4. Discover a person who attended college in the northeastern United States.
   Name: _____
   Job description: _____

5. Discover a person who owns a laptop computer.
   Name: _____
   Job description: _____

6. Discover a person who plays golf.

   Name: _____

   Job description: _____

7. Discover a person who enjoys watching "Jeopardy" on television.

   Name: _____

   Job description: _____

8. Discover a person who consults the Weather Channel on television.

   Name: _____

   Job description: _____

9. Discover a person who speaks a foreign language.

   Name: _____

   Job description: _____

10. Discover a person who has traveled in a foreign country.

    Name: _____

    Job description: _____

Activity 1.9
TEST YOUR INGENUITY

Objective: To stress the importance of collaboration, pooling of different perceptions, and creative thinking in problem-solving

Estimated Time: 15 to 20 minutes

Materials Needed: Handout 1.9: Test Your Ingenuity (one copy for each group); list of answers for facilitators (below)

Directions for Facilitators

1. Organize participants into groups of four.
2. Explain to them that the activity will give them an opportunity to collaborate, think creatively, and have fun.
3. Distribute one copy of the handout to each group. Each numbered frame represents a phrase or popular saying. Solve the first frame together to make sure all participants understand the process. Tell them they will have 15 minutes to solve the puzzles.
4. After 15 minutes, ask for volunteers to reveal the answers. (Refer to the answer list provided.)

Answers to Test Your Ingenuity, Activity 1.9

1. Crazy over you
2. Making ends meet
3. Deep-sea fishing
4. Teetotaler
5. It's a small world after all
6. She's beside herself
7. Three degrees below zero
8. Close quarters
9. Space invaders
10. Adding insult to injury
11. Call it a day
12. Downtown
13. The odds are overwhelming
14. Just between you and me
15. You are under oath
16. Time's up

Handout 1.9
TEST YOUR INGENUITY

Directions for Participants

1. Each numbered square represents a phrase or popular saying.
2. Collaborate, think creatively, and solve all the puzzlers within 15 minutes.
3. Prepare to volunteer to reveal your answers.

1. <u>CRAZY</u>
   YOU
	2. END
	   N
	   D
		3. FISHING
		
		   C
			4. T
			
			   T
			
			   T
			   —
			   3T

5.
 	
ALL world
	6.
	
	She's Herself
		7. <u>O</u>
		
		   B.A.
		
		   Ph.D.
		
		   M.D.
			8.
			
			$\frac{1}{4}$ $\frac{1}{4}$ $\frac{1}{4}$ $\frac{1}{4}$

9. VAD ERS	10. Injury + Insult	11. 24 Hours	12. T
			
			   O
			
			   W
			
			   N

13. 13579
WHELMING
	14. You Just Me	15. <u>OATH</u>
		   UR
			16. M M
			   A P

Handout 1.9.   Permission is granted to photocopy for classroom use.

SELF-ASSESSMENT

This section provides nonthreatening activities that allow individual participants to explore their own attitudes toward homosexuality and the development of sexual feelings. For some participants, this may be the first time they will have formally focused on this kind of introspection.

The activities in this section have been designed to help workshop participants establish a personal frame of reference before they examine, as the workshop progresses, the attitudes, ideas, beliefs, and feelings of others.

Activity 2.1: Self-Exploration involves a personal attitude development questionnaire on homosexuality to help participants focus on their own feelings. The purpose of Activity 2.2: Developmental Aspects of Sexuality is to generate discussion regarding the evolution of an individual's sexuality. (Background information for facilitators is provided for this activity.) Activity 2.3: Self-Assessment Inventory focuses participants' attention on the development of their individual sexuality. A general discussion follows to enhance self-awareness and to sensitize participants to the feelings of others. Activity 2.4: Belief Statements Regarding Gays and Lesbians calls on participants to examine some of the beliefs concerning gays and lesbians that have been promoted by some of the significant people in their lives, such as parents, relatives, teachers, and religious leaders. This activity becomes a self-assessment as participants determine their degree of agreement or disagreement with the identified beliefs.

Activity 2.1
SELF-EXPLORATION

Objective: To assist individuals in identifying how their feelings toward homosexuality evolved so that they can enhance their sensitivity and awareness of how other people's attitudes toward homosexuality developed. (The purpose of this activity is self-exploration and not disclosure to others.)

Estimated Time: 10 to 15 minutes

Materials Needed: Handout 2.1: Homosexuality Attitude Development Questionnaire (one copy for each participant)

Directions for Facilitators

1. Distribute Handout 2.1 to all participants.
2. Read the following directions to participants: "I am handing out a form with some questions to help you better understand how your attitudes toward homosexuality developed. Please complete this form as honestly as you can. This may not be as easy an activity as you might expect it to be. If you need any clarification about these questions, please do not hesitate to ask for assistance. This information is very personal and confidential and will not be disclosed to anyone else unless you choose to do so. You will have 10 to 15 minutes to complete this form."
3. After participants complete the activity, explain to them that this was a self-exploratory activity to examine their feelings regarding homosexuality. Emphasize that personal self-disclosure during the workshop is not necessary.

Key Points for Facilitators to Elicit

1. Know yourself and explore how your feelings developed.
2. There is no uniform feeling. Everyone feels differently, depending on his or her own experiences and his or her perception of those experiences.

Handout 2.1
HOMOSEXUALITY ATTITUDE
DEVELOPMENT QUESTIONNAIRE

Directions for Participants

Please complete this form as honestly as you can. This information is very personal and confidential and will not be disclosed to anyone else unless you choose to do so.

1. At what age were you first aware of homosexuality?

2. What are your earliest memories concerning the topic of homosexuality and how did/do you feel about them?

3. Identify other experiences that you have had that may validate or refute these feelings?

4. How have your feelings changed as you have acquired more knowledge and information about homosexuality?

5. What helped modify your attitude change?

Activity 2.2
DEVELOPMENTAL ASPECTS OF SEXUALITY

Objective: To generate discussion and share information regarding the development of sexual feelings
Estimated Time: 20 to 30 minutes
Materials Needed: Easel, markers, chart pad

Directions for Facilitators

1. Prepare the following questions for discussion on the facilitators' chart pad:

    At what age do people become aware of sexual feelings?
    Are these feelings constant or do they change over time? What stimulates them?
    How are feelings of sexuality expressed?
    What type of response may be generated by the expression of sexuality?
    How do these early feelings impact children as they become adults?

2. Organize participants into groups of four to six members.
3. Ask each group to choose a leader whose task will be to generate discussion concerning the questions on the chart pad and to identify some responses that can be shared with the larger group. (Allow 10 minutes to complete this exercise before coming to the larger group for discussion.)
4. Call on each leader for individual group feedback.

BACKGROUND INFORMATION

By the time children are three years old, they are able to accurately identify themselves as boys or girls and have some concept of what this means. During the early childhood years of five to eight, children develop an increased sensitivity to the role differences between girls and boys. They compare and contrast their feelings with what they observe and learn from their friends, siblings, and parents. For some children, it is at this early age that they begin to feel different from some of their peers.

A sense of sexual identity begins to emerge more strongly with the onset of puberty. During adolescence, teenagers begin to have a stronger sense of their feelings and who they are. Teenagers may respond by either accepting their feelings and learning to express them or denying and repressing their feelings. For many adolescents, this is a very difficult time and may be fraught with many emotional ups and downs. They may be confused about what is happening to them, physically and emotionally. They may begin sharing their feelings with peers and others and react strongly to the responses they receive. At times such disclosure may be difficult, because peer acceptance and approval is important at this stage and teenagers are not always comfortable fully disclosing their feelings and may have few people they trust.

Dating begins and some sexual experimentation may occur. Teenagers' self-images are strongly affected by their dating experiences, and their sexual feelings and perceptions from these experiences will frequently persist throughout their lives. Once a negative self-image develops, it is very difficult to modify this perception. It requires a concerted effort. This will strongly impact social relationships, both in their private lives and in their interactions with others at work. It is not uncommon for adults who are successful in their careers to maintain their early negative self-perceptions of body image and self-consciousness in interpersonal relationships. Feelings of sexuality can be expressed in various ways: through verbal messages, such as the language and intonation of what is being said; through dress, such as suggestive or tight-fitting clothes or loose-fitting, nonsexual attire to mask their sexuality; through behaviors that send strong signals of "come close" or "stay away." If people feel confident and good about who they are, they can feel more positive and successful in their relationships with others. Sexual identity and positive feelings about oneself contribute greatly to relationships with others. This is true for both heterosexuals and homosexuals. The two cases that follow are illustrative of experiences some teenagers have.

John

John was fifteen when he first had the confidence to ask a girl for her phone number. He was a tall, skinny teenager with a severe case of acne. Despite the fact that he was an honor student, he felt he could not do anything right. During his high school years, as he repeatedly was turned down for dates from the girls he pursued, he began to socially isolate himself and feel even more awkward and uncomfortable in his interpersonal interactions with girls. He had few friends and revealed his feelings and fears to no one. John did not succeed in establishing a long-term heterosexual relationship until he was in his mid-twenties.

Bob

John's story is quite a contrast to Bob, a handsome seventeen-year-old male who was the most popular guy on his high school campus. He always had a plethora of people, especially girls, desiring his company. Yet he felt he did not "belong" and thought he was a phony. He wondered if he would still be popular if people knew he were gay. His self-esteem was poor and he spent his teenage years believing he was a fraud.

Background Information for Activity 2.2.   Permission is granted to photocopy for classroom use.

Activity 2.3
SELF-ASSESSMENT INVENTORY

Objective: To explore how participants' feelings of sexuality developed, in order to increase their sensitivity and awareness of how other people's sexuality develops

Estimated Time: 25 to 30 minutes

Materials Needed: Handout 2.3: Self-Assessment Questionnaire (one copy for each participant)

Directions for Facilitators

1. Distribute one copy of Handout 2.3 to each participant with the following instructions: "I am passing out a questionnaire for each of you to complete. It contains very personal questions, but you will not have to share your answers with anyone else. The purpose of this activity is to assist you in examining your own feelings of sexuality and how they developed. It is believed that by increasing your awareness regarding how you developed your feelings, it will make it easier for you to understand and respond to other people's feelings of sexual development." (Allow 15 minutes for this part of the activity.)

2. When the questionnaire has been completed, initiate a discussion among participants by using some or all of the questions provided. If no discussion is generated, personalize for the group in the following way: "Many times we don't think about how our attitudes and beliefs are formulated or how we acquired these feelings. The focal point of this exercise is to enhance self-awareness and sensitivity so we can be more aware of others."

Questions for Discussion

1. How comfortable were you with this activity?
2. Was this easy or difficult to complete?
3. Did this bring out any new or uncomfortable feelings?
4. How comfortable would you feel sharing these feelings with others? (*Note:* the participants do not need to share their feelings, just the fact of how comfortable they would feel sharing their feelings.)
5. How comfortable do you think you would have felt discussing these issues as a teenager?

6. Do you think this increased personal awareness may help influence your attitude, reactions, or work with young people?
7. Do you think these feelings should be explored with adolescents? If so, how?
8. What suggestions do you have for educators to help adolescents address these issues?

Key Points for Facilitators to Elicit

1. Discussing the development of sexual feelings is not easy.
2. Many people do not spend time exploring the origins of their sexual feelings.

Handout 2.3
SELF-ASSESSMENT QUESTIONNAIRE

Directions for Participants

1. Please realize that answers to the following questions will *not* have to be shared with anyone else.
2. Use these questions to assist you in examining your own feelings of sexuality and how they developed.
3. Answer each question as honestly as you can. Keep the answers to yourself.
(*Reminder: This information is personal and will not be shared with anyone else.*)

1. How do you identify yourself sexually: as a homosexual, heterosexual, bisexual, or asexual?

2. How did you arrive at this determination and at what age?

3. When did you first become aware of your sexual feelings?

4. How did you feel about this? Was this okay, or did you feel uncomfortable?

5. How comfortable did you feel with your peers as an adolescent? a young adult? today?

6. Does any aspect of your sexuality have anything to do with your comfort level with others? Peers? Siblings? Family members? Friends? Others?

7. Do you think your sexual feelings affected your learning experiences when you were in school, or your participation in extracurricular activities?

8. Do you think your sexual feelings have affected your work or interactions with others at work?

9. How old were you when you remember receiving your first sexual messages? From whom did you receive them?

10. What verbal/nonverbal messages about sex did your parents convey?

11. How comfortable were you with these messages?

12. How did you assimilate these messages in your life?

13. Was there a special person in your life who helped make you aware of your sexuality? Why was this person so special and how did he/she help influence you? How does this affect your feelings and lifestyle today?

14. Did your sexual feelings ever get you in trouble as an adolescent or as an adult? If yes, what could have helped you to avoid this difficulty?

15. How old were you when you had your first sexual experience?

16. Were you comfortable with this experience? Do you feel you were ready for this experience? If not, what could have helped make you more ready?

17. Do your feelings of love seem similar or different from your peer group? Why?

18. How comfortable are you today discussing your feelings of sexuality? With whom would you be comfortable discussing this and why?

19. What messages do you feel young people should receive about sexuality?

20. Who should provide young people with this information and how should this information be presented?

Activity 2.4
BELIEF STATEMENTS REGARDING
GAYS AND LESBIANS

Objective: To focus participants on the origins of beliefs they have encountered concerning gays and lesbians

Estimated Time: 25 to 30 minutes

Materials Needed: Handout 2.4: Belief Statements Regarding Gays and Lesbians (one copy for each participant)

Directions for Facilitators

1. Distribute Handout 2.4 to all participants.
2. Ask participants to follow directions on the handout. Tell them they will have approximately 15 minutes to complete the activity.
3. Upon completion of the activity, initiate discussion by asking volunteers to answer the following question: "What generalizations can you make from examining your chart?" Use some of the following examples of generalizations to help facilitate the discussion if there is limited group participation:

    "My beliefs about homosexuals have changed a lot since I was a
      teenager."
    "My grandmother had absolutely no clue about homosexuality."
    "My beliefs about gays and lesbians have not changed since I was a
      teenager."
    "The minister in our town was a bigot, but I didn't realize it when I was
      a kid."

Key Points for Facilitators to Elicit

1. Beliefs people hold may not always be based on facts.
2. People should explore their feelings before they strongly incorporate them into their personal belief system.
3. Many varied belief systems are strongly upheld by many people.

Handout 2.4
BELIEF STATEMENTS REGARDING
GAYS AND LESBIANS

Directions for Participants

1. In column 1 of the chart that follows, list five beliefs you have encountered in your lifetime regarding gays and lesbians. These beliefs may be positive or negative. (This information will not be shared with anyone in the workshop.)
2. Determine the person(s) who advocated the beliefs and write a one-word description of that person(s) in column 2 (see example on the chart).
3. Fill in columns 3 and 4 using the following keys:

Column 3: Method used by the person(s) to transmit the belief

   I = Imposition (The person moralized about the issue or imposed his/her belief.)

   M = Modeling (The individual(s) personified the belief by the way he/she lived his/her life.)

Column 4: Degree of agreement or disagreement

SA = strongly agree
SD = strongly disagree
N = neutral or don't know
PA = partially agree
PD = partially disagree

Beliefs Concerning Gays and Lesbians:	The Person(s) Who Advocated the Belief:	Methods Used By the Person(s) to Transmit the Belief:	Degree of My Agreement or Disagreement:
EXAMPLE: Diverse sexual orientations are a sin	Minister	I	SA
Belief A:			
Belief B:			
Belief C:			
Belief D:			
Belief E:			

Handout 2.4. Permission is granted to photocopy for classroom use.

ORIGINS OF HOMOSEXUALITY

Most people have an opinion regarding the causes of homosexuality; some of these opinions are research based, others are not. It is essential for workshop participants to be familiar with research-based knowledge before they are exposed to the remaining sections of the workshop. This section reviews the three major theories concerning the cause(s) of homosexuality: environmental, genetic, and psychological. In addition, it presents a summary of the most recent data collected by geneticists supporting the possibility of a genetic basis for homosexuality. Activity 3.1: What Causes Homosexuality? provides an opportunity for participants to speculate about the origins of homosexuality. In Activity 3.2: Understanding the Origins of Homosexuality the facilitators share with the participants the theoretical constructs regarding the origins of homosexuality. The major purpose is to promote an understanding of the various theories. Activity 3.3: Facts about Homosexuality includes a questionnaire for participants to complete. The Background Information for Facilitators provides information that supports or refutes the items on the questionnaire. In addition, questions are given for facilitators to pose as each item on the questionnaire is discussed with participants. Activity 3.4: Famous Gays and Lesbians stimulates thought and discussion regarding stereotyping and the idea that the only characteristic distinguishing homosexuals from the heterosexual population is sexual orientation.

Activity 3.1
WHAT CAUSES HOMOSEXUALITY?

Objective: To identify the origins of homosexuality
Estimated Time: 15 to 20 minutes
Materials Needed: None

Directions for Facilitators

1. Organize participants into groups of six.
2. Instruct them to answer the following question and to produce a written statement that best summarizes their group members' feelings. Question: "What causes homosexuality? or What are the origins of homosexuality?" (Allow 10 minutes for this part of the activity.) Each group will select a leader who will share the group's answer with all workshop participants.
3. When participants have completed their responses, elicit the report from each group. (Focus discussion on the similarities and differences among the responses and see if the entire group can arrive at a consensus. If consensus is not attainable, identify those factors that prevent this from occurring, such as the topic being too controversial or lack of information, etc.)

Key Points for Facilitators to Elicit

1. Obtaining consensus on the causes of homosexuality is not easy, as there are varying opinions.
2. The scientific evidence on the subject suggests a genetic cause, but this is not yet definitive.

Activity 3.2
UNDERSTANDING THE ORIGINS OF HOMOSEXUALITY

Objective: To promote an understanding of the different theories regarding the causes of homosexuality
Estimated Time: 30 to 45 minutes
Materials Needed: Handout 3.2: Origins of Homosexuality (one copy for each group)

Directions for Facilitators

1. Discuss Background Information with participants. (This presentation should take approximately 10 to 15 minutes.)
2. Organize participants into four groups, distribute one copy of Handout 3.2 to each group, and assign a different question to each group to discuss. (Allow 15 minutes for discussion.)
3. Ask one member from each group to share its question and responses with all participants.

Key Points for Facilitators to Elicit

1. A number of theories have been advanced explaining the origins of homosexuality. While the genetic theory is gaining greater acceptance, it still has not been definitively proven.
2. Homosexuality is part of the human condition.

BACKGROUND INFORMATION

Few issues raise the passion and intensity of discussion and disagreement as trying to identify the causes and origins of homosexuality. There are three primary theories about the cause of homosexuality: environmental, genetic, and psychological. Although no theory has gained wide acceptance among the broad population, researchers are lending greater support to the possibility of a genetic basis for homosexuality.

Historical Perspectives

In studying previous cultures and civilizations and reviewing the earliest writings that have been found, Tripp (1987) has found that homosexuality is prevalent in many cultures and is predominant in some. The environmental theory purports that boys who masturbate at an early age establish positive feelings and relationships between their maleness and their male genitalia, which becomes very arousing and desirable. This leads to an attraction to and desire to be with other males. Additional variables include a negative initial experience with someone of the opposite sex, which leads to a preference for someone of the same sex.

In New Guinea, the Kwai require young men to be sodomized during puberty rites to make them strong. This practice is similarly done by the Papuans and Keraki. Following their exile from Babylonia, the Hebrews practiced religious fellatio. It is believed these early sexual practices may have facilitated a same-sex preference and acceptance.

In societies where homosexuality is a matter of free choice, it rarely disappears. In eastern Peru, an isolated branch of the Amarakaer was predominantly homosexual, with heterosexual contacts occurring on only two or three ceremonial occasions a year. These heterosexual encounters were completed quickly and did not appear to be demonstrations of affection.

Among various North American Indian tribes, when a young boy was recognized as being effeminate he was labeled a *berdache* (man-woman) and would be trained and treated as though he were a woman. Among the Siberian Chuchee, it was common for a man to have several female wives and one male wife who dressed and acted like a woman in all respects. In Moslem societies, where there is a distinct separation of the sexes, there has been an increase in the practice of homosexuality. This does not hold true in all societies. For example, in Hindu societies, the lowest rates of homosexuality occur with the highest degree of female segregation.

Tripp (1987) found much evidence to suggest a society's concept of maleness and the values attached to it are what most control the degree of homosexuality. The virtues ascribed to men in most tribes and civilizations are similar; but there are large differences in the kinds of qualities expected of males and in their individual responses. In societies where homosexuality was rare, once it was introduced, it tended to very quickly become an accepted and common practice.

Biological Factors

A growing body of research (Hamer, Hu, Magnuson, Hu, & Pattatucci, 1993; Pool, 1993) is beginning to identify a link between a small segment of DNA on the X chromosome and some cases of male homosexuality. Hamer et al. studied 76 homosexual men and found 13.5% of them had homosexual brothers. Upon further investigation, they found more gay relatives on the maternal than paternal side. It seemed more prevalent in maternal uncles of gay men and among cousins who were sons of maternal aunts than in males in the general population. They suspected the cause might be a gene on the X chromosome. Hamer et al. then studied 40 pairs of homosexual brothers and found that 33 pairs shared a set of five markers on the end of the long arm of the X chromosome called Xq28. They believed a gene in this area may be the one that predisposes a male to become homosexual.

In 1978 Gorski, Gordon, Shrine, and Southam were investigating rat brains and found that one group of cells near the front of the hypothalamus was several times larger in male rats than in female rats. Gorski and his colleagues found that dimorphic structures in the human brain in a cell group named INAH3 (third interstitial nucleus of the anterior hypothalamus) were three times larger in men than women. In 1991 LeVay examined the hypothalamus in autopsy specimens from 19 homosexual men, 16 heterosexual men, and 6 women whose sexual orientation was unknown, all of whom died of AIDS. He found that INAH3 was more than twice as large in men as in women and between two and three times larger in straight men than in gay men.

In 1986 Pillard and Weinrich studied patterns of homosexuality within families. They found that 57% of identical twins, 24% of fraternal twins, and 13% of brothers of gay men are also gay. In women they found 50% of identical twins, 16% of fraternal twins, and 13% of sisters of lesbians are lesbian. As described above, Hamer et al. (1993) later confirmed these findings by determining that a brother of a gay man had a 14% likelihood of being gay, as compared with 2% for a man without a gay brother. Maternal uncles were found to have a 7% chance of being gay and maternal aunts an 8% chance.

Gender Identification

Developmentally, by the time children reach the age of three, they begin to identify and label themselves as either a girl or a boy and are aware of the differences between the two genders. Attempts at modifying their identification at this age are very difficult. Green (1987) followed 44 "feminine" boys for a 15-year period to determine if "feminine behavior" was an indicator of homosexuality. He found "sissy" boys played girl-type games, dressed in girl's clothing, played with girls, and expressed strong desires to be a girl. Kagan and Moss (1962) also conducted a 25-year study of personality and gender role development from childhood to adulthood and found a high correlation between boys' childhood "feminine" behavior and interests and adult gender role behaviors and interests.

Children form gender identification based on the feelings and messages they get from others. They gradually learn which behaviors and actions are affiliated with males and females. Eventually they become more comfortable with their gender identity. For some young children, however, this may not be an easy time because they may feel different from others and not have a forum for being able to express these feelings. Attempts at doing so may arouse uncomfortable and negative responses from their families or others. Therefore, they may begin to feel confused and uncertain. They do not understand why they do not feel the way they think they are supposed to feel. This can lead to lowered self-esteem, confusion, anxiety, depression, withdrawal, and isolation from others.

Kinsey, Pomeroy, and Martin (1948) believed that an important turning point for male homosexuality occurs at the onset of puberty. They found a high positive correlation between an earlier onset of puberty and the frequency of adolescent and adult homosexuality. This relationship did not seem to exist with lesbians. Kinsey et al. believed sexual behavior is reinforced by high sexual drives, which for males occurs between the ages of 16 and 20.

Psychological Theories

Freud (1963) believed homosexuality results from a child's relationship with his or her parents being interrupted at a developmentally early age. Freud believed that at the age of four or five the young child formed a strong attachment to the parent of the opposite sex. He described this as being the Oedipal stage of development. He believed if, during this stage of development, there was no strong male figure for a young boy, this child would form a strong attachment to his mother that he could not act on, and would therefore suppress his feelings for his mother and direct his feelings toward other men. He believed that homosexuality could be treated by modifying a male's perception by working through his attachment to his mother.

According to Freud (1963), another psychological cause of homosexuality is a child's inability to establish a strong relationship with a same-sex parent. Therefore, feelings that would have been resolved in the parental relationship become transferred to other individuals of the same sex. Freud believed the child would try to gain the acceptance from a same-sex individual that he or she was unable to attain with the same-sex parent.

Other theories have stated the cause of homosexuality is the absence of a strong father figure and the presence of a dominant mother figure. Isay (1985, 1986, 1987) found many gay adult males lacked close bonds with their fathers in childhood because of distortions in their early attachments to them. He believed a normal developmental issue for boys was to adopt cross-gender behavioral characteristics in order to acquire and sustain their fathers' attention.

Social learning theorists believe there is a combination of factors that can contribute to the development of homosexuality. These theorists believe, through observation of the male and female roles in society, children acquire stereotypic behavior and become more comfortable with their own identity. As children move into adolescence this becomes further solidified by their interaction with others, the sexual messages they receive through both verbal and physical contact, and the comfort level they feel in these interactions. It is important for children and adolescents to find social groups in which they feel comfortable. Once this is acquired the individuals may begin to label themselves as homosexual.

Identity Formation

There has been a growing body of literature dealing with the development of identity formation. Troiden (1989) has been at the forefront in this area and has developed a four-stage model of homosexual identity formation: sensitization, identity confusion, identity assumption, and commitment. Sensitization occurs at an early stage of development, usually before the onset of puberty. Many homosexuals do not recognize this as a developmental stage, because they may not realize they are homosexual, even though they may experience feelings of being different. Being "different" does not mean they are homosexual at this stage.

During the next stage, identity confusion, adolescents begin to examine their feelings and behaviors more closely and begin to recognize that they may be homosexual. This may be a particularly trying time, because adolescents also have to reconcile the messages and feelings they have received about homosexuality with the recognition that they may be homosexual. Adolescents respond to these feelings with either denial, avoidance, redefinition of themselves, or acceptance.

During the identity assumption stage adolescents begin to become more comfortable with their homosexuality and may even begin to "come out" to other homosexuals in safe settings. In the final stage, commitment, individuals finally feel comfortable admitting to themselves that they are homosexual and accept the sexual orientation as a way of life. Gradually, they may become comfortable disclosing their sexual identity to heterosexuals as well.

References

Freud, S. (1963). Certain neurotic mechanisms. In *Sexuality and the psychology of love* (pp. 150–160). New York: Collier.

Gorski, R., Gordon, J., Shrine, J., & Southam, A. (1978). Evidence for a morphological sex difference within the medial pre-optic area of the rat brain. *Brain Research, 148*, 333–346.

Green, R. (1987). *The "sissy boy syndrome" and the development of homosexuality.* New Haven, CT: Yale University Press.

Hamer, D., Hu, S., Magnuson, V., Hu, N., & Pattatucci, A. (1993, July 16). A linkage between DNA markers on the X chromosome and male sexual orientation. *Science, 261*, 321–327.

Isay, R. (1985). On the analytic therapy of homosexual men. *Psychoanalytic Study of the Child, 40*, 235–254.

Isay, R. (1986). The development of sexual identity in homosexual men. *Psychoanalytic Study of the Child, 41*, 467–489.

Isay, R. (1987). Fathers and their homosexually inclined sons in childhood. *Psychoanalytic Study of the Child, 42*, 275–294.

Kagan, J., & Moss, H. A. (1962). *Birth to maturity.* New York: Wiley.

Kinsey, A. C., Pomeroy, W. B., & Martin, C. E. (1948). *Sexual behavior in the human male.* Philadelphia: W. B. Saunders.

LeVay, S. (1991, August 30). A difference in hypothalamic structure between heterosexual and homosexual men. *Science, 253*, 1034–1037.

Pillard, E., & Weinrich, J. (1986). Evidence of familial nature of male homosexuality. *Archives of General Psychiatry, 43*, 808–812.

Pool, R. (1993). Evidence for homosexuality gene. *Science, 261*, 291–292.

Tripp, C. (1987). *The homosexual matrix* (2nd ed.). New York: Meridian.

Troiden, R. R. (1989). The formation of homosexual identities. *Journal of Homosexuality, 17*(1–2), 43–73.

Background Information for Activity 3.2.   Permission is granted to photocopy for classroom use.

Handout 3.2
ORIGINS OF HOMOSEXUALITY

Directions for Participants

1. Discuss the assigned question from below within your group for 15 minutes.
2. One member of your group should prepare to share your question and responses with all participants.

1. Why do some segments of the general population reject a genetic basis for homosexuality? Do you feel there is enough evidence to support the notion of a "gay gene"?
2. Why do you think the general population tends to be more accepting of an environmental cause of homosexuality?
3. If the "gay gene" theory is demonstrated to be a valid theory, how do you think this will influence and modify the general population's beliefs and behaviors toward homosexuality? Should governmental laws and policies be changed?
4. If the causes of homosexuality are environmental, what can/should be done to modify the beliefs about and actions toward gays and lesbians? If environment is the origin, what types of behavioral engineering should be initiated?

Handout 3.2.   Permission is granted to photocopy for classroom use.

Activity 3.3
FACTS ABOUT HOMOSEXUALITY

Objective: To provide participants with facts to dispel myths about homosexuality
Estimated Time: 55 to 60 minutes
Materials Needed: Handout 3.3: Questionnaire: Facts about Homosexuality (one copy for each participant)

Directions for Facilitators

1. Read Background Information in preparation for discussion of the questionnaire. All questions have been answered in the Background Information section with supporting evidence and questions for discussion.
2. Distribute one copy of Handout 3.3 to all participants and ask them to complete it. (Allow 5 minutes for this activity.)
3. Address each item on the questionnaire and present relevant statistics to support or refute each item. Following each presentation, open the floor for a brief discussion and use the questions provided to encourage group participation.

Key Points for Facilitators to Elicit

1. Gather data before assuming myths are facts or vice versa.
2. Homosexuality is no longer classified as a mental illness.
3. Homosexuals are not always easily identifiable and many are no different from everyone else. They are employed in all occupations.
4. There are no clear-cut causes for homosexuality.
5. Homosexuality cannot be changed.

BACKGROUND INFORMATION

1. Homosexuality is an emotional illness.

In the 1970s the American Psychological Association and the American Psychiatric Association amended their previous positions that homosexuality is an emotional illness and rejected this notion. They clarified their feelings by stating that homosexuals may become emotionally ill from being persecuted or being forced to hide their sexual orientation from society. At its January 1975 meeting the American Psychological Association Council adopted the following policy statement regarding discrimination against homosexuals:

> 1. The American Psychological Association supports the action taken on December 15, 1973 by the American Psychiatric Association, removing homosexuality from that Association's official list of mental disorders. The American Psychological Association therefore adopts the following resolution:
> Homosexuality, per se, implies no impairment in judgment, stability, reliability, or general social or vocational capabilities:
> Further, the American Psychological Association urges all mental health professionals to take the lead in removing the stigma of mental illness that has long been associated with homosexual orientations.
> 2. Regarding discrimination against homosexuals, the American Psychological Association adopts the following resolution concerning their civil and legal rights: The American Psychological Association deplores all public and private discrimination in such areas as employment, housing, public accommodation, and licensing against those who engage in or who have engaged in homosexual activities and declares that no burden of proof of such judgment, capacity, or reliability shall be placed upon these individuals greater than that imposed on any other person. Further, the American Psychological Association supports and urges the enactment of civil rights legislation at the local, state, and federal levels that would offer citizens who engage in acts of homosexuality the same protections now guaranteed to others on the basis of race, creed, color, etc. Further, the American Psychological Association supports and urges the repeal of all discriminatory legislation singling out homosexual acts by consenting adults in private. (American Psychological Association, 1975, p. 633)

The research of the past two decades has not been able to verify any substantiative psychological, genetic, or hormonal uniformity among homosexuals or heterosexuals.

Questions for Discussion

1. Why do you think homosexuality had been classified as a mental illness?
2. What do you think may have caused the American Psychological Association and American Psychiatric Association to modify their opinions?
3. Why do you feel homosexuality should or should not be classified as a mental illness?

2. Homosexuals are easily identifiable.

A perpetuated myth is that gay men are effeminate and lesbians are masculine. Although there certainly are individual homosexuals who satisfy this perception, the majority of homosexuals do not. There also are many heterosexual males who are effeminate and heterosexual females who are masculine. The majority of homosexuals do not act, dress, or in any other manner distinguish themselves from the rest of the population. Berger, Hank, Rauzi, and Simkins (1987) asked gay and lesbian individuals to identify, by looking at people they did not know, whether these individuals were gay or lesbian; 71% of the gay men and 44% of the lesbians believed they could identify someone's sexual orientation solely by looking at them. Only 20% of them exceeded chance levels in correctly detecting homosexuals.

Questions for Discussion

1. What behaviors, attitudes, or appearance do you think identifies someone as a homosexual?
2. How frequently do you assume someone is a homosexual? How accurate have you been in your assessments? Why do you speculate on someone's sexual orientation?
3. What constitutes femininity? Masculinity?
4. Why do you think some individuals engage in deliberate actions to make themselves appear homosexual?

3. Homosexuality can be changed.

According to the American Psychiatric Association ("Attempts to Cure Homosexuality," 1994), there is no public scientific evidence that supports the effectiveness of therapy to modify sexual orientation. In fact, mental health professionals who try to cure adolescents of homosexuality against their will can be prosecuted. For years, therapists employed techniques such as aversive conditioning, which involved administering a mild electrical stimulation to the individual when he or she had homosexual thoughts; psychoanalysis, which focused on trying to modify the parent-child relationship; and antiandrogen drugs, which altered sexual hormonal levels and often caused asexuality. Although some individuals appear to change as a result of such interventions, some of this change may be due to individuals making a choice that they wish to pursue heterosexual relationships, based on an exploration of their personal feelings and moving toward a lifestyle in which they feel comfortable.

There are several groups that advocate homosexuality can be changed. The belief is that homosexuality is caused by a gender-inferiority complex that originates sometime during early childhood and can be modified. Two of these groups are the Exodus Ex-Gay Ministries and the Evergreen Foundation, a nonprofit group of former homosexuals, which advocates that homosexuality can be cured thorough sports and therapy.

Questions for Discussion

1. Why do you think individuals might want to change their sexual orientation?
2. How do you think they might feel if they tried to change their orientation and were unsuccessful?
3. What do you think can be done to make individuals more accepting of their sexual orientation?

4. Acting like a sissy or a tomboy can cause homosexuality.
Green (1987) spent 15 years following 44 "feminine" boys from childhood to adulthood. He found that "sissy" boys frequently expressed wishes to be girls throughout their childhoods, played with girls exclusively, played girl-type games, and often dressed in girls' clothing. Many of these behaviors were also subtly encouraged by the boys' parents through laughter, sharing of these actions with other family members and friends, and taking pictures and videos of these actions. Although Green was unable to demonstrate that these responses contributed to the development of homosexuality, he concluded that feelings of inadequacy, low self-esteem, and confusion regarding one's sexual identity did arise.

Questions for Discussion

1. Can you identify what constitutes "sissy" or "tomboy" behavior?
2. Do you think this should be labeled as homosexual behavior? Why? Why not?

3. What are acceptable messages for parents to give their children regarding "sissy" or "tomboy" behavior?

5. Homosexuals are employed primarily in certain occupations.

Homosexuals can be found in virtually every career field. Although several fields have been more commonly associated with homosexuals, such as theater professionals, hairdressers, clothing designers, and interior decorators, this myth may have been perpetuated because many homosexuals have decided to remain closeted in other occupations for fear of discrimination and potential loss of employment. Many incidents have been documented in which individuals have been terminated from positions, or attempts at termination have occurred, once their sexual orientation became public knowledge.

One of the most predominant cases in the education field occurred in 1969 when the California Supreme Court reviewed the *Morrison v. State Board of Education* case and ruled that extensive analysis of an individual's behavior in relation to his or her job responsibilities was necessary before employment dismissal could occur. Being homosexual was not sufficient grounds for dismissal unless it was associated with some other related misbehavior (Harbeck, 1991). In 1974, a case in Montgomery, Maryland (*Acanfora v. Board of Education of Montgomery County*) resulted in a teacher being terminated from his position because he had lied on his job application about his political activities as a homosexual. Although the rights of gays and lesbians and of teachers is protected by the First Amendment, the judge permitted Acanfora's dismissal because he had lied on his job application. Acanfora said he did not fully reveal his political activities because he was afraid he would not be hired.

In 1991 eleven employees were dismissed from the Cracker Barrel Old Country Store because they were gay or perceived to be gay (Mickens, 1994). There is no federal law that prevents private employers from refusing to hire, fire, or undercompensate homosexuals solely because of the person's sexual orientation, regardless of aptitude or work record.

A highly controversial situation occurred in the military in August 1992. Keith Meinhold publicly revealed his homosexuality and was discharged from the Navy after having served for 14 years. In November 1992, a federal judge ruled the military ban on gays and lesbians unconstitutional and ordered Meinhold reinstated. Meinhold left the military in the Spring of 1996, after 16 years of service (Komarow, 1997). Another case that drew much attention was that of Margarethe Cammermeyer, a National Guard colonel, who was terminated after her sexual orientation was revealed to an investigator in 1989 while she was being interviewed for a top security clearance job. She was reinstated as of April 1994, when the judge ruled her discharge violated the constitutional guarantee of equal protection.

The three most common job categories for gay men are management, health care, and education. Forty percent more gays and lesbians are employed in the fields of finance and insurance than in the arts. Ten times as many gays and lesbians work with computers as work in the fashion industry (Fefer, 1991).

Questions for Discussion

1. Should homosexuals be allowed to openly express their sexual orientation in school and workplace settings?
2. What guidelines should be instituted to ensure that homosexuals can be employed in all occupations?
3. Are there occupations for which you feel sexual orientation should be a consideration for employment?

6. Homosexual parents will raise homosexual children.

Bozett (1987) reviewed more than 30 studies comparing children of homosexual parents with those of heterosexual parents and found no significant differences in terms of gender identity or sexual orientation. Schulenburg (1985) also reported that children of homosexual parents have about the same chance of being homosexual as the children of heterosexuals. Homosexual children appear to come primarily from heterosexual parents.

Researchers have found that children of gay and lesbian parents have no more frequent psychiatric problems and gender dysfunction than do children of heterosexual parents (Golombok, Spencer, & Rutter, 1983; Green, 1987; Hoeffer, 1981; Hotvedt & Mandel, 1982; Kirkpatrick, Smith, & Roy, 1981; Miller, Mucklow, Jacobsen, & Bigner, 1980; Pagelow, 1980) Daughters of lesbian mothers worry more about becoming homosexuals than do sons (Pennington, 1987). This may occur because girls are more aware of their emerging sexuality and their strong identification with their mothers. Sons of lesbians do not seem to be as concerned about their own sexual identification and relationships with girls, because they do not strongly identify with their mother's sexuality. Children of gay fathers tend to use social control strategies to ensure that others do not think they are gay and seem able to separate their father's sexual orientation from the role of fatherhood (Bozett, 1987).

Schulenburg's (1985) research found fewer than 10% of gay and lesbian parents felt their children were unhappy or resentful of their sexual identification and more than 30% reported their children were happy and proud of their parents. If gay and lesbian parents are comfortable with themselves and their sexuality, the children seem more able to accept their parents' homosexuality. Many children seem to acquire their ideas regarding their parents' sexual identification from their parents' attitudes and beliefs.

Questions for Discussion

1. What are some concerns people have about homosexuals as parents?
2. How valid are these concerns?
3. What steps can be taken to address these concerns?
4. Do you feel homosexuals should have the right to adopt children?
5. Do you feel homosexuals should be involved in activities that involve children, such as Boy Scouts, teaching, camp counselors, etc.?

7. The majority of child molesters are homosexual.

According to Paul, Weinrich, Gonsiorek, and Hotvedt (1982), recognized researchers in the fields of child abuse and law enforcement, homosexuals are less likely than heterosexuals to approach children. The majority of child molesters are heterosexual. Groth and Birnbaum (1978) found that child molesters tend to be hostile toward homosexuals. Freund, Langevin, Cibiri, and Zajac (1973) measured sexual arousal in homosexual and heterosexual males in response to various erotic displays. They found homosexuals were not as sexually aroused by photos of little boys as heterosexual males were by photos of little girls. These researchers concluded that homosexuals are less likely than heterosexuals to be involved in acts of child molestation.

Questions for Discussion

1. Why, contrary to statistical information, does the public view child molesters as homosexual?
2. What can be done to change the public's perception that child molesters are primarily homosexual?
3. How do you feel about groups such as the North American Man/Boy Love Association (NAMBLA), a group of adult males that encourages gay men to have sexual relationships with young boys? What type of regulation do you think should be legislated for groups of this type?

8. Homosexuals cannot maintain long-term relationships.

This belief has probably arisen because of the myth that homosexuals frequent seedy bars and bath houses in search of brief sexual interludes. Researchers

(Bell & Weinberg, 1978; Peplau, 1983/1984) have concluded that many homosexuals lead stable lives and are involved in long-term relationships. Many gay couples are beginning to exchange vows and are lobbying for the legal right to marry and be given the same benefits and rights as domestic partners that heterosexual spouses have. As of September 1993, 25 jurisdictions in the United States recognized homosexual relationships (Rubenstein, 1993).

Questions for Discussion

1. What can or should the gay community do to dispel the belief that homosexuals are unable to maintain long-term relationships?
2. Why is the heterosexual community not thought of this way when the divorce rate is around 50%? Shouldn't this lead to a similar conclusion that heterosexuals are unable to maintain long-term relationships?
3. What can be done to modify people's misperceptions about the gay community?

9. Homosexuals have abandoned organized religion.

Because many sects within organized religion have advocated that homosexuality is sinful, the belief is that homosexuals have abandoned organized religion. Many homosexuals were raised in households where religion and the values of religion were part of their upbringing. They miss the sense of community and connection with a higher power that traditional religion offers. With the formation of the Metropolitan Community Church (MCC) in 1968, many gays and lesbians began to return to organized religion. Today there are more than 290 MCC churches in seventeen countries reaching out primarily to Christian homosexuals. There is a growing religious movement among Jewish homosexuals, United Gay and Lesbian Christian Scientists, homosexual Episcopals (Integrity), Jehovah's Witnesses (Sovereignty), Mormons (Affirmation), and Methodists (also known as Affirmation). With greater acceptance within traditional churches some homosexuals also are returning to their local churches where they are being welcomed by primarily heterosexual congregations. Also, many clergymen are beginning to perform same-sex marriages and are acknowledging the desire for a lifetime commitment between same-sex partners. In March 1996, at the central conference of American Rabbis, representing Reform rabbis, an overwhelming majority supported a resolution endorsing gay and lesbian civil marriage.

Questions for Discussion

1. Do you feel homosexuals should be welcome in traditional organized religion?

2.   Why do you feel religion has excluded homosexuals?
3.   What suggestions would you have that would encourage homosexuals and heterosexuals to belong to the same churches?

10.   Having one or several homosexual experiences makes a person a homosexual.
The popular belief is that homosexuality is defined as any sexual activity that occurs between members of the same sex. This narrow definition of homosexuality does not account for the fact that during adolescence it is not uncommon for teenagers to experiment sexually, and to have a single or several homosexual episodes. This does not necessarily mean a teenager who experiences these episodes will become a homosexual. Kinsey, Pomeroy, and Martin (1948) reported approximately one third of all males admitted to having at least one post-pubertal orgasmic experience with another male. According to Blumenfeld and Raymond (1993), there is much controversy among researchers in the social sciences as to when in history people began to construct their personal lives around same-sex attractions. The school of "essentialism" believes gays and lesbians have always existed and have been present in most civilizations. "Constructivism" assumes that a break in thinking occurred in the 19th century that enabled a "homosexual identity" to emerge. According to Blumenfeld and Raymond, being gay or lesbian is more than sexual behavior alone. It includes attitudes, values, and lifestyle choices and having an affectional preference or orientation for members of one's own sex.

Questions for Discussion

1.   What behaviors or feelings should identify someone as a homosexual or a heterosexual?
2.   What are some parameters that are used to label someone as homosexual or heterosexual?
3.   At what age do you believe individuals realize whether they are homosexual or heterosexual?
4.   Is sexual experimentation part of the process of validating whether an individual is homosexual or heterosexual?

References

Acanfora v. Board of Education of Montgomery County, 359 F. Supp. 846 (District Court, Montgomery County, MD, 1974).

American Psychological Association. (1975). Proceedings of the American Psychological Association for the year 1974. *American Psychologist, 30*, 620–651.

Attempts to cure homosexuality could mean litigation. (1994, June 13). *Mental Health Weekly, 4*(23), 1–2.

Bell, A. P., & Weinberg, M. S. (1978). *Homosexualities: A study of diversity among men and women.* New York: Simon & Schuster.

Berger, G., Hank, L., Rauzi, T., & Simkins, L. (1987). Detection of sexual orientation by heterosexuals and homosexuals. *Journal of Homosexuality, 13*(4), 83–100.

Blumenfeld, W. J., & Raymond, D. (1993). *Looking at gay and lesbian life* (2nd ed.). Boston: Beacon Press.

Bozett, F. W. (Ed.). (1987). *Gay and lesbian parents.* New York: Praeger.

Fefer, M. (1991, December 16). Gay in corporate America. *Fortune,* 42–54.

Freund, K., Langevin, R., Cibiri, S., & Zajac, Y. (1973). Heterosexual aversion in homosexual males. *British Journal of Psychiatry, 122,* 163–169.

Golombok, S., Spencer, A., & Rutter, M. (1983). Children in lesbian and single parent households: Psycho-sexual and psychiatric appraisal. *Journal of Child Psychology & Psychiatry, 24*(4), 551–572.

Green, R. (1987). *The "sissy boy syndrome" and the development of homosexuality.* New Haven, CT: Yale University Press.

Groth, A. N., & Birnbaum, H. J. (1978). Adult sexual orientation and attraction to underage children. *Archives of Sexual Behavior, 7,* 175–181.

Harbeck, K. M. (1991). Gay and lesbian educators: Past history/future prospects. *Journal of Homosexuality, 22,* 121–139.

Hoeffer, B. (1981). Children's acquisition of sex-role behavior in lesbian-mother families. *American Journal of Orthopsychiatry, 51* (31), 536–543.

Hotvedt, M., & Mandel, J. (1982). Children of lesbian mothers. In W. Paul, J. D. Weinrich, J. C. Gonsiorek, & M. E. Hotvedt (Eds.), *Homosexuality: Social, psychological and biological issues* (pp. 275–285). Beverly Hills, CA: Sage.

Kinsey, A. C., Pomeroy, W. B., & Martin, C. E. (1948). *Sexual behavior in the human male.* Philadelphia: W. B. Saunders.

Kirkpatrick, M., Smith, C., & Roy, R. (1981). Lesbian mothers and their children: A comparative study. *American Journal of Orthopsychiatry, 51*(3), 545–551.

Komarow, S. (1997, February 27). *USA Today*, p. 4A.

Mickens, E. (1994, April 9). Waging war on Wall Street. *The Advocate*, 40–45.

Miller, J. A., Mucklow, B. M., Jacobsen, R. B., & Bigner, J. J. (1980). Comparison of family relationships: Homosexual vs. heterosexual women. *Psychological Reports, 46*, 1127–1132.

Pagelow, M. (1980). Heterosexual and lesbian single mothers: A comparison of problems coping and solutions. *Journal of Homosexuality, 5*, 189–205.

Paul, W., Weinrich, J. D., Gonsiorek, J. C., & Hotvedt, M. E. (Eds.) (1982). *Homosexuality: Social, psychological and biological issues*, Beverly Hills, CA: Sage.

Pennington, S. B. (1987). Children of lesbian mothers. In F. W. Bozett (Ed.), *Gay and lesbian parents* (pp. 58–74). New York: Praeger.

Peplau, L. A. (1983/1984). What homosexuals want. In O. Pocs (Ed.), *Human sexuality* (pp. 201–207). Guilford, CT: Dushkin Publishing.

Rubenstein, W. B. (Ed.). (1993). *Lesbians, gay men and the law*. New York: The New Press.

Schulenburg, J. A. (1985). *Gay parenting: A complete guide for gay men and lesbians with children*. Garden City, NY: Anchor Books.

Background Information for Activity 3.3.   Permission is granted to photocopy for classroom use.

Handout 3.3
QUESTIONNAIRE: FACTS ABOUT HOMOSEXUALITY

Directions for Participants

1. Read each statement and circle "T" for true or "F" for false, based on your personal feelings and knowledge about homosexuality. (You will have 5 minutes to answer all the questions.)
2. Please be ready to enter into discussion on each item.

1. Homosexuality is an emotional illness.   T   F
2. Homosexuals are easily identifiable.   T   F
3. Homosexuality can be changed.   T   F
4. Acting like a sissy or a tomboy can cause homosexuality.   T   F
5. Homosexuals are employed primarily in certain occupations.   T   F
6. Homosexual parents will raise homosexual children.   T   F
7. The majority of child molesters are homosexual.   T   F
8. Homosexuals cannot maintain long-term relationships.   T   F
9. Homosexuals have abandoned organized religion.   T   F
10. Having one or several homosexual experiences makes a person a homosexual.   T   F

Activity 3.4
FAMOUS GAYS AND LESBIANS

Objective: To stimulate thought and discussion about gay and lesbian occupational stereotypes

Estimated Time: 20 to 25 minutes

Materials Needed: Handout 3.4 (Part A): Famous Gays and Lesbians and Handout 3.4 (Part B): Answer Key to Famous Gays and Lesbians (one copy of each for each group)

Directions for Facilitators

1. Organize participants into groups of four.
2. Distribute Handout 3.4 (Part A) (one copy to each group). (*Note*: The list of Famous Gays and Lesbians was compiled from scholarly biographical sources and public announcements made by some of the persons themselves.)
3. Ask each group to collaborate and complete the matching activity within 15 minutes.
4. After time has been called, distribute Handout 3.4 (Part B) (one copy to each group). Ask each group to compare its answers with the answer key.
5. After each group has checked its answers, use the questions provided to stimulate general discussion.

Questions for Discussion

1. What were some of your personal reactions or comments to one another as you completed this activity?
2. What can be learned from this activity?

Handout 3.4 (Part A)
FAMOUS GAYS AND LESBIANS

Directions for Participants

1. Discuss the items below among group members for 15 minutes.
2. Match the famous people listed in column A with the appropriate description in column B.

Column A	Column B
1. ___ Julius Caesar	A. British author
2. ___ Dag Hammarskjöld	B. Mathematical/ computer genius
3. ___ David Kopay	C. Olympic gold medal swimmer
4. ___ Roberta Achtenberg	D. British author and mathematician
5. ___ Barney Frank	E. Colonel, U.S. National Guard
6. ___ Richard C. Failla	F. Attorney/former Assistant Director of U.S. Housing & Urban Development
7. ___ Lewis Carroll	G. American author
8. ___ Alan Turing	H. U.S. congressman (Massachusetts)
9. ___ Debra A. Batts	I. New York Supreme Court justice
10. ___ James Baldwin	J. U.N. secretary general
11. ___ John Maynard Keynes	K. Professional football player
12. ___ Margarethe Cammermeyer	L. State legislator (Minnesota)
13. ___ Karen Clark	
14. ___ Virginia Woolf	
15. ___ Greg Louganis	
16. ___ Peter the Great	
17. ___ Walt Whitman	
18. ___ Alexander the Great	
19. ___ Bruce Hayes	
20. ___ Susan Love	

M. Federal judge
N. British economist
O. American poet
P. Roman emperor
Q. Russian czar
R. Physician, breast cancer activist
S. Olympic diving gold medalist
T. Macedonian ruler

Handout 3.4 (Part A). Permission is granted to photocopy for classroom use.

Handout 3.4 (Part B)
ANSWER KEY TO FAMOUS GAYS AND LESBIANS

Directions for Participants

1. Within your group compare your answers with the answers below.
2. Discuss those items where your responses differ from the answer key.

Column A   Column B

1. P Julius Caesar
2. J Dag Hammarskjöld
3. K David Kopay
4. F Roberta Achtenberg
5. H Barney Frank
6. I Richard C. Failla
7. D Lewis Carroll
8. B Alan Turing
9. M Debra A. Batts
10. G James Baldwin
11. N John Maynard Keynes
12. E Margarethe
       Cammermeyer
13. L Karen Clark
14. A Virginia Woolf
15. S Greg Louganis
16. Q Peter the Great
17. O Walt Whitman
18. T Alexander the Great
19. C Bruce Hayes
20. R Susan Love

A. British author
B. Mathematical/
   computer genius
C. Olympic gold
   medal swimmer
D. British author and
   mathematician
E. Colonel, U.S.
   National Guard
F. Attorney/former
   Assistant Director
   of U.S. Housing &
   Urban Development
G. American author
H. U.S. congressman
   (Massachusetts)
I. New York Supreme
   Court justice
J. U.N. secretary
   general
K. Professional football
   player
L. State legislator
   (Minnesota)
M. Federal judge

N. British economist
O. American poet
P. Roman emperor
Q. Russian czar
R. Physician, breast cancer activist
S. Olympic diving gold medalist
T. Macedonian ruler

HOMOPHOBIA

Homophobia is the single most important factor preventing the understanding of people with a different sexual orientation. It is responsible for much violence, discrimination, fear, suppression of human potential, and death.

The activities in this section acquaint workshop participants with the history, causes, types, effects, consequences, and prevention of homophobia. Activity 4.1: Homophobia: Significant Historical Events defines the concept of homophobia and presents a brief historical overview of events that have led to present-day homophobic laws and attitudes. (Background Information for Facilitators is provided for this activity.) The purpose of Activity 4.2: Motivations for Homophobic Thought and Behavior is to stimulate thinking and discussion about what motivates homophobic thought and behavior in today's society. Activity 4.3: Fact or Myth? presents a questionnaire to stimulate discussion relative to the myths that perpetuate homophobic attitudes. Activity 4.4: Types of Homophobia acquaints participants with three different types of homophobia and promotes discussion on how homophobia manifests itself within the educational environment. Activity 4.5: The Impact of Homophobia on Gay and Lesbian Youth presents four separate readings that illustrate how homophobia affects gay and lesbian youth.

Activity 4.6: Effects of Homophobia Experienced by Gay and Lesbian Students creates an awareness and sensitivity among participants regarding the effects of homophobia experienced by gay and lesbian students in educational settings. (The authors recommend that this activity be supported by a videotape or audiotape selected from the resource list in Section XII.) Activity 4.7: Readings and Discussion provides student testimonials and an excerpt that address the duty of school administrators to make a safe environment available to all students. Activity 4.8: Educating to Reduce and Prevent homophobia encourages participants to be proactive in their schools to reduce and prevent homophobia. The activity establishes a list of specific actions that can be taken in educational set-tings to prevent and/or reduce homophobia. Activity 4.9: Beliefs Concerning Gays and Lesbians consists of an inventory of beliefs relating to gays and lesbians that gives participants the opportunity to discuss and compare their beliefs with other members of the workshop. Activity 4.10: Consequences of Actions Relative to Gays and Lesbians focuses on five common behaviors and their positive and negative consequences.

Activity 4.1
HOMOPHOBIA: SIGNIFICANT HISTORICAL EVENTS

Objective: To define the concept of homophobia and trace historical occurrences that have led to present-day homophobia
Estimated Time: 15 to 20 minutes
Materials Needed: None

Directions for Facilitators

Using the Background Information, define homophobia for the participants and provide a brief historical overview of some important events that have influenced present-day homophobic laws and attitudes.

BACKGROUND INFORMATION

Homophobia is defined as an intense fear or hatred of gays and lesbians that includes various levels of prejudice, discrimination, or aggression. Homophobia has a long history; it is not just a 20th-century phenomenon. Beginning with the early Greek and Roman civilizations, religious, social, philosophical, and political attitudes laid the groundwork for intolerance of homosexuality in European and some Latin American countries. Among the penalties were execution (by burning, hanging, drowning, and stoning) and various forms of dismemberment. After the French Revolution of 1789, the death penalty was abolished in France and liberalized penalties prevailed in French colonies.

England abolished the death penalty for homosexuals in the mid-19th century, but new laws prohibited same-sex acts between consenting adults in public or private and provided penalties of imprisonment. These laws prevailed until 1967 when the Wolfenden Report was responsible for the removal of laws prohibiting homosexual acts between consenting adults in private.

Germany had severe penalties for homosexuality until the mid-20th century. During the early 1900s attempts were made by a few German scientists and intellectuals to promote the removal of the antihomosexual "Paragraph 175" from the German penal code, which made homosexual acts a criminal offense; these liberal attempts failed to make a difference in German law. With the rise of Fascism and the domination of the Nazi party, an antihomosexual campaign was launched and resulted in violent attacks against individuals and organizations dedicated to the legal reform of the penal code. The Nazis strengthened the laws against homosexual behavior, which gave them license to hunt, torture, and incarcerate suspected homosexuals. Eventually, the Third Reich was successful in rounding up an estimated 100,000 men whom they arrested and charged with the crime of homosexuality. Most of these men were sent to regular prisons and concentration camps where many were tortured or murdered.

Early American colonists adopted English laws concerning homosexuality. Even after the American Revolution ended Britain's domination over the American colonies, many of the inherited British laws were not changed, including laws against homosexuality. Such laws imposed harsh penalties, and there are documented cases of executions carried out in the colonies. Since the late 18th century, individual U.S. states have passed their own laws regulating homosexual behavior. In some states laws do exist to protect the rights of gays and lesbians; in other states a person can be imprisoned or legally denied housing, child custody, employment, public accommodations, or inheritance on the basis of his or her sexual orientation.

As we approach the 21st century, homophobia continues to be a dominant characteristic of American society, resulting in harassment, violence, and death. Worldwide, many countries continue to legally impose harsh penalties, including the death penalty, for homosexual behavior.

Background Information for Activity 4.1.   Permission is granted to photocopy for classroom use.

Activity 4.2
MOTIVATIONS FOR HOMOPHOBIC
THOUGHT AND BEHAVIOR

Objective: To stimulate thought and discussion about homophobia and establish a composite list of motivations
Estimated Time: 35 to 40 minutes
Materials Needed: Chart paper, easel, markers

Directions for Facilitators

1. Organize participants into groups of six.
2. Ask each group to establish and chart a list, based upon consensus, of motivations for homophobic thought and behavior. Each group should select a leader who will post the chart and report to the full group of participants.
3. Encourage discussion after each leader has presented. (Allow 15 to 20 minutes for this activity.)
4. Chart a composite list of motivations and post it conspicuously, where it should remain throughout the section of the workshop on homophobia. If the following motivations do not appear on any of the group charts, they should be mentioned by the facilitators and included on the composite list:

    *   fear of differences,
    *   personal insecurities and inadequacies,
    *   assuming the prejudices of others to effect a sense of community,
    *   individual feelings of failure,
    *   protection of one's sense of self-esteem,
    *   reduction of feelings of personal guilt,
    *   confusion regarding one's own sexual orientation,
    *   generalizing from an isolated negative incident with a gay or lesbian, and
    *   subtle "teaching" of homophobia by parents and other significant people.

Activity 4.3
FACT OR MYTH?

Objective: To help participants think about, identify, and discuss some of the common myths that perpetuate homophobic thinking

Estimated Time: 40 to 50 minutes

Materials Needed: Handout 4.3: Questionnaire: Fact or Myth? (one copy for each group)

Directions for Facilitators

1. Read Background Information in preparation for discussion of the questionnaire. All questions have been answered in the Background Information section with supporting evidence and questions for discussion.
2. Organize participants into groups of six.
3. Distribute one copy of Handout 4.3 to each group.
4. Instruct participants to choose one person in each group to read each statement aloud and lead the group through discussion to a consensus for each statement. (Allow 20 minutes for discussion.)
5. After all groups have completed the questionnaire, review the answers by calling on each group leader to report three or four responses until all statements have been discussed.

(Correct responses: Items 1–5 = myth; items 6 and 7 = fact; items 8–11 = myth)

BACKGROUND INFORMATION

1. Most gays and lesbians can be identified by their mannerisms, dress, and/or appearance.

In 1987, Berger, Hank, Rauzi, and Simkins studied the ability of gay men and lesbians to identify the sexual orientation of strangers; 71% of gay men and 44% of lesbians believed they could accurately discern an individual's sexual orientation on the basis of looks, mannerisms, and appearances. The results showed only 20% exceeded chance levels of correct identification. Therefore, if individuals who are homosexual have difficulty making an accurate determination, the likelihood of heterosexuals making an accurate assessment of sexual orientation also may be minimal.

2. In homosexual relationships, one partner is always "male" and the other "female."

According to numerous researchers (Bem, 1974, 1975; Block, 1973; Harry & DeVall, 1978; Heilbrun, 1976; Peplau, 1983/1984; Saghir & Robbins, 1973; Spence & Helmreich, 1978), there seems to be an equal relationship between homosexual partners. The dichotomy of male and female behaviors does not appear to exist.

3. Homosexuality is an emotional illness caused by poor parenting and other environmental factors not conducive to "normal" sexual development.

In the 1970s both the American Psychological Association and the American Psychiatric Association adopted resolutions stating homosexuality is not a mental illness. They concurred that individuals can become emotionally ill from being unable to express their sexual orientation or being persecuted because of it. Although many theories are espoused regarding the development of sexuality, there is no clear evidence to indicate that homosexuality results from poor parenting.

4. Homosexuals are clannish and they all stick together.

People who share common interests and belief systems frequently spend more time together. Similarities between people help cement relationships. That explains why individuals of similar religions, occupations, sports interests, or sexual orientation might gravitate to one another. There is no documented evidence that homosexuals are any more "clannish" than the heterosexual population.

5. Gays and lesbians are oversexed and indiscriminately promiscuous.

Promiscuous individuals are present in both the heterosexual and homosexual communities; however, there is no clear evidence to support the notion that gays and lesbians are oversexed and indiscriminate in their choice of partners.

6. Parents reject their sons and daughters on the basis of sexual orientation.

In one study, half of all lesbian and gay youth interviewed reported their parents rejected them because of their sexual orientation (Remafedi, 1987).

7. Homosexuals cannot be trusted with national secrets.

For almost 50 years official federal discrimination has existed against lesbians and gay men in the government. Since 1947 federal employees have been screened for trustworthiness and loyalty before having clearance for access to classified information. In 1953, "sexual perversion" was added as a basis for firing federal workers, and since then various agencies have used that standard to label homosexuals as security risks. The rationale was that federal employees who kept their homosexuality secret were vulnerable to blackmail by foreign agents, who could threaten the federal workers with exposure if they did not cooperate. On August 4, 1995, President Clinton officially ended the government assumption that homosexuals cannot be trusted with national secrets by issuing an executive order halting discrimination based on sexual orientation in granting security clearance ("Clinton Ends Anti-Gay Security Bias," 1995).

8. Lesbians and gays are unfit as teachers and can influence their students' sexual orientation.

In most parts of the United States, lesbian and gay teachers cannot reveal their sexual orientation without jeopardizing their jobs. Therefore, few studies have been done regarding the effects of gay and lesbian teachers. However, neurobiological research of the early 1990s indicates that sexual orientation is determined either before birth or very early in life and that no one can alter another person's sexual orientation.

In a study of 161 homosexual males with twin or adoptive brothers, 52% of the subjects' identical twin brothers, 22% of their fraternal twin brothers, and 11% of their adoptive brothers were homosexual, supporting the theory of a biological link (Bailey & Pillard, 1991). A study of lesbian twin sisters found similar results: The identical twins of lesbians were three times more likely to be lesbian or bisexual than were the fraternal twins (Bailey, 1993).

LeVay (1991) compared the brain tissue of 19 homosexual and 16 heterosexual men and found a significant difference between the two groups in a cluster of cells in the hypothalamus (a region involved in sexual response).

In a study of 979 homosexual and 477 heterosexual men, most said their sexual orientation was established before adolescence, regardless of whether they had been sexually active at that time (Bell, Weinberg, & Hammersmith, 1991).

There is no evidence that gay and lesbian teachers' effectiveness in the classroom differs from that of heterosexual teachers.

In a psychological test that predicts the success of teachers in the classroom, administered to 74 gay and lesbian and 66 heterosexual teachers, no differences in scores between the two groups were found (Martin, 1990).

In the case of *Morrison v. the State Board of Education*, 1969, the Supreme Court of California ruled that the state could not revoke the teaching license of a homosexual teacher unless it could demonstrate "unfitness to teach" with factual evidence rather than with a presumption of "immorality" (Hunter, Michaelson, & Stoddard, 1992).

In 1974, the National Education Association (the nation's largest organization of public school employees) added "sexual orientation" to its resolution on nondiscriminatory personnel policies and practices that it urges its members' employers to follow.

9. Most gays and lesbians tend to congregate in "seedy" bars and restaurants.
The percentage of homosexuals who frequent gay and lesbian bars with regularity is estimated to be between 10 and 25% (Gonsiorek & Weinrich, 1991). According to *Bob Damron's Address Book* (1993), there are 1,672 lesbian and gay bars in the United States. These statistics do not support the notion that most gays and lesbians tend to congregate in "seedy" bars and restaurants. Most homosexuals desire close long-term relationships with their partners and their families. In a 1992 study, 55.5% of gay men and 71.2% of lesbians reported being involved in steady relationships (Overlooked Opinions, 1992). These statistics are comparable to those found by Peplau (1983/1984) where he found 60% of lesbians and 40% of gay men were in long-term relationships.

10. Most teachers or employers are able to identify the students/workers in their classrooms/workplaces who are gay and lesbian.
As explained for the first statement, the identification of individuals' sexual orientation is not usually easily achieved. Therefore, most teachers or employers are unable to successfully identify gay or lesbian students/workers.

11. Gays or lesbians can change to be heterosexuals.
There are several organizations that claim that homosexuality can be changed. The Evergreen Foundation, an organization of former homosexuals, believes that homosexuality can be modified through sports and therapy. They believe homosexuality develops from a gender inferiority complex that occurs in early childhood and that this attitude can be changed. Exodus Ex-Gay Ministries also supports the notion that homosexuals can change their sexual orientation. The beliefs of these organizations have not been substantiated by researchers. According to the American Psychiatric Association, there is no evidence to support the effectiveness of therapy to modify one's sexual orientation ("Attempts to Cure Homosexuality," 1994).

12. Acts of violence against gays and lesbians is an infrequent occurrence.

According to Comstock (1991), more than half of all socially active gay men and lesbians have experienced some violence. Most of these incidents have occurred in public places frequented by gay men or lesbians, such as bars or community centers. Most of the perpetrators, responsible for 50% of all reported incidents, were 21 years of age or younger, of which 94% were male. Approximately two thirds of the perpetrators did not know their victims. Acquaintances and policemen were the second and third most common perpetrators of antigay and antilesbian violence. In 1988 40% of the 500 lesbian, gay, and bisexual youths who visited the Hetrick-Martin Institute for services reported having experienced violent attacks (Herek & Berrill, 1992).

13. Domestic benefits are legally mandated for homosexual partners.

The National Gay and Lesbian Task Force sent surveys to the 1,000 largest companies in the United States in 1993. Of that group, 757 companies did not respond at all and 145 companies specifically refused to comply with the survey. Of the 98 companies that returned the survey, only five offered domestic-partner benefits to same-sex partners (Singer & Deschamps, 1994). Levi Strauss and Company, which employs 23,000 workers, was the largest company in 1992 offering health insurance to same-sex domestic partners (Woods & Lucas, 1993). According to a December 1994 newspaper article (Weiner, 1994), more than 140 public and private employers are extending medical benefits to gay and lesbian domestic partners. There is, however, as yet no legal mandate for such coverage.

14. Gay/lesbian clubs are offered on many school and college campuses.

In 1993 there were more than 100 lesbian and gay support groups in high schools across the country (Dorning, 1993). Gay clubs are gaining greater visibility on college campuses. As of January 1992, 15 colleges had gay/lesbian task forces, 43 offered some courses, and 248 had nondiscrimination policies regarding sexual orientation (Singer & Deschamps, 1994). On April 18, 1996, the Utah legislature passed a bill to ban gay/lesbian student clubs in Utah high schools. The bill is the only one of its kind in the nation to win passage.

References

Attempts to cure homosexuality could mean litigation. (1994, June 13). *Mental Health Weekly, 4*(23), 1–2.

Bailey, J. M. (1993). Heritable factors influence sexual orientation in women. *Archives of General Psychiatry, 50*, 217–223.

Bailey, J. M., & Pillard, R. A. (1991, December). Genetic study of male sexual orientation. *Archives of General Psychiatry, 48,* 1089–1096.

Bell, A. P., Weinberg, M. S., & Hammersmith, S. K. (1981). *Sexual preference: Its development in men and women.* Bloomington, IN: Indiana University Press.

Bem, S. (1974). The measurement of psychological androgyny. *Journal of Consulting & Counseling Psychology, 42,* 155–162.

Bem, S. (1975). Sex-role adaptability: One consequence of psychological androgyny. *Journal of Personality & Social Psychology, 31,* 634–643.

Berger, G., Hank, L., Rauzi, T., & Simkins, L. (1987). Detection of sexual orientation by heterosexuals and homosexuals. *Journal of Homosexuality, 13*(4), 83–100.

Block, J. H. (1973). Conceptions of sex role: Some cross-cultural and longitudinal perspectives. *American Psychologist, 28,* 512–526.

Clinton ends anti-gay security bias. (1995, August 5). *The Atlanta Journal/The Atlanta Constitution,* 8A.

Comstock, G. (1991). *Violence against lesbians and gay men.* New York: Columbia University Press.

Damron, B. (1993). *The 29th edition of Bob Damron's address book.* San Francisco: Author.

Dorning, M. (1993, November 30). School's support groups helping gay teens to cope. *Chicago Tribune.*

Gonsiorek, J., & Weinrich, J. (1991). *Homosexuality: Research implications for public policy.* Newbury Park, CA: Sage.

Harry, J., & DeVall, W. (1978). *The social organization of gay males.* New York: Praeger.

Heilbrun, A. B. (1976). The measurement of masculine and feminine sex role identities as independent dimensions. *Journal of Consulting Psychology, 44,* 143–190.

Herek, G., & Berrill, K. (Eds.). (1992). *Hate crimes: Confronting violence against lesbians and gay men.* Newbury Park, CA: Sage.

Hunter, N. D., Michaelson, S. E., & Stoddard, T. B. (1992). *The rights of lesbians and gay men: The basic ACLU guide to a gay person's rights.* Carbondale, IL: Southern Illinois University Press.

LeVay, S. (1991, August 30). A difference in hypothalamic structure between heterosexual and homosexual men. *Science, 253,* 1034–1037.

Martin, M. (1990). *Gay, lesbian, and heterosexual teachers: Acceptance of self, acceptance of others.* Unpublished report.

Overlooked Opinions. (1992, January). *The gay market.* Chicago: Author.

Peplau, L. A. (1983/1984). What homosexuals want. In O. Pocs (Ed.), *Human sexuality* (pp. 201–207). Guilford, CT: Dushkin Publishing.

Remafedi, G. (1987). Male homosexuality: The adolescent's perspective. *Pediatrics, 79,* 326–330.

Saghir, M., & Robbins, E. (1973). *Male and female homosexuality: A comprehensive investigation.* Baltimore: Williams & Wilkins.

Singer, B. L., & Deschamps, D. (Eds.). (1994). *Gay and lesbian stats: A pocket guide of facts and figures.* New York: The New Press.

Spence, J., & Helmreich, R. (1978). *Masculinity and femininity: Their psychological dimensions, correlates, and antecedents.* Austin: University of Texas Press.

Weiner, H. (1994, December 28). More companies adding benefits for partners of gays and lesbians. *Miami Herald,* 8C.

Woods, J., & Lucas, J. (1993). *The corporate closet: The professional lives of gay men in America.* New York: The Free Press.

Background Information for Activity 4.3.   Permission is granted to photocopy for classroom use.

Handout 4.3
QUESTIONNAIRE: FACT OR MYTH?

Directions for Participants

1. Choose one person in your group to be the spokesperson.
2. Have the spokesperson read each statement aloud to the group and allow time for discussion.
3. Seek consensus and then circle "F" for fact and "M" for myth. (You will have 20 minutes to complete this exercise.)

1. Most gays and lesbians can be identified by their mannerisms, dress, and/or appearance.   F   M
2. In homosexual relationships, one partner is always "male" and the other "female."   F   M
3. Homosexuality is an emotional illness caused by poor parenting and other environmental factors not conductive to "normal" sexual development.   F   M
4. Homosexuals are clannish and they all stick together.   F   M
5. Gays and lesbians are oversexed and indiscriminately promiscuous.   F   M
6. Parents reject their sons and daughters on the basis of sexual orientation.   F   M
7. Homosexuals cannot be trusted with national secrets.   F   M
8. Lesbians and gays are unfit as teachers and can influence their student's sexual orientation.   F   M
9. Most gays and lesbians tend to congregate in "seedy" bars and restaurants.   F   M
10. Most teachers or employers are able to identify the students/workers in their

classrooms/workplaces who are gay
and lesbian.   F   M
11.   Gays or lesbians can change to be
heterosexuals.   F   M
12.   Acts of violence against gays and
lesbians is an infrequent occurrence.   F   M
13.   Domestic benefits are legally mandated
for homosexual partners.   F   M
14.   Gay/lesbian clubs are offered on many
school and college campus.   F   M

Handout 4.3.   Permission is granted to photocopy for classroom use.

Activity 4.4
TYPES OF HOMOPHOBIA

Objective: To acquaint participants with three different types of homophobia and give them the opportunity to discuss how homophobia is manifested within the academic environment
Estimated Time: 25 to 30 minutes
Materials Needed: Handout 4.4: Types of Homophobia (one copy for each participant), chart paper, and markers for participants; masking tape

Directions Facilitators

1. Organize participants into groups of six.
2. Distribute Handout 4.4 to all participants and ask them to read the directions and follow instructions as noted.
3. Stimulate discussion as each group leader presents. If participants overlook certain examples of institutional homophobia, initiate discussion to include the following:

   - the lack of support services for gay and lesbian students;
   - the lack of positive role models for gay and lesbian students;
   - the silence of educational personnel when derogatory terms are used;
   - the absence of honest discussions of homosexuality in health and sex education classes;
   - the subtle discrimination against gay and lesbian educational personnel;
   - not acknowledging famous gays and lesbians in various curriculum areas;
   - the absence of appropriate gay and lesbian print and nonprint materials in media centers and guidance offices;
   - the absence of training for school personnel concerning how to meet the needs of gay and lesbian students;
   - the absence of school policies protecting gay and lesbian students from harassment, violence, and discrimination; and
   - the absence of support for families of gay and lesbian students.

Questions for Discussion

1. In your institution, which factors of homophobia are present and how are they manifested?

2. Have there been efforts to effect change in your institution? If yes, what? If no, what suggestions would you have for implementing change?

Key Points for Facilitators to Elicit

1. There are three types of homophobia.
2. Personal homophobia may be the most difficult to modify and affects interpersonal and institutional homophobia.
3. Homophobia is manifested in different ways within various academic environments.

Handout 4.4
TYPES OF HOMOPHOBIA

Directions for Participants

1. Read the information below concerning the three types of homophobia.
2. Select a person to facilitate the discussion within your group and prepare lists of examples delineating each type of homophobia. Present the group's lists to all workshop participants during the discussion. (Your group will have approximately 15 minutes to compile its lists.)

1. *Personal homophobia* involves the personal belief that gays and lesbians are any or all of the following: inferior to heterosexuals, mentally ill, sinners, immoral, and unacceptable in society. Sometimes it involves the fear of being considered gay or lesbian, regardless of one's sexual orientation, and thus being subjected to stereotyping and hostility.
2. *Interpersonal homophobia* involves a fear or hatred of people believed to be gay or lesbian. This fear or hatred may be expressed through discrimination or various degrees of aggression.
3. *Institutional homophobia* involves the ways that social institutions, such as government, religious organizations, businesses, and schools discriminate against people (sometimes in subtle ways) on the basis of sexual orientation.

List 1: Specific examples of interpersonal homophobia expressed by individuals within school settings.

List 2: Specific examples of institutional homophobia (expressed or unexpressed) that exist within school settings.

Handout 4.4. Permission is granted to photocopy for classroom use.

Activity 4.5
THE IMPACT OF HOMOPHOBIA ON GAY
AND LESBIAN YOUTH

Objective: To provide documented information regarding homophobia and youth
Estimated Time: 20 to 25 minutes
Materials Needed: Handout 4.5: How Gay and Lesbian Youth Are Impacted by
Homophobia (4 copies)

Directions for Facilitators

1.   Distribute the copies of Handout 4.5 to four volunteer participants.
     Assign one reading to each volunteer.
2.   Ask them to read the selections to the entire group.
3.   Facilitators should encourage discussion after each reading.

Key Points for Facilitators to Elicit

1.   There are many students in distress who go unnoticed by educators.
2.   Educators and parents need to take an active role in effecting change.
3.   Pay attention to the signals students send.

Handout 4.5
HOW GAY AND LESBIAN YOUTH ARE
IMPACTED BY HOMOPHOBIA

Directions for Participants

1. Read aloud the assigned reading from below.
2. Discuss the reading using the suggested questions.

Reading 1

"I just began hating myself more and more, as each year the hatred towards me grew and escalated from just simple name-calling in elementary school to having persons in high school threaten to beat me up, being pushed and dragged around the ground, having hands slammed in lockers, and a number of other daily tortures." (Steven Obuchowski, 18, testifying at the public hearings of the Massachusetts Governor's Commission on Gay and Lesbian Youth, 1992)

Questions for Discussion

1. How do you think Steven felt about school and his classmates?
2. How do you think these actions affected Steven's self-concept? academic behavior? social relationships?
3. How do you think Steven will be affected as an adult?
4. What interventions could have assisted Steven?
5. What suggestions do you have for other students in similar situations?
6. What can be done to increase awareness among educators and prevent these situations from occurring?

Reading 2

"Suicide is the leading cause of death for gay and lesbian adolescents.

There is an epidemic of youth suicide in the U.S. today.

500,000 youths try to kill themselves EACH YEAR. Between 1950 and 1980, there was a 170% increase in suicides of people between the ages of 15 and 24.

Gay and lesbian youth are 2 to 3 times more likely to attempt suicide than their peers.

Gay and lesbian youth comprise 30% of completed youth suicides."

[Feinleib, M. R. (Ed.). (1989). *Report of the secretary's task force on youth suicide: Prevention and interventions in youth suicide*. Washington, DC: U.S. Department of Health and Human Services.]

Questions for Discussion

1. How do you feel about these statistics?
2. What interventions can assist youth in school? in the community? in family interactions? with peers?
3. What are some of the warning signs of suicidal thoughts and potential actions?

Reading 3

"Studies such as those by Professor Gregory Herek of the University of California–Davis have shown that the key factor in reducing fear and intolerance of gays and lesbians is a positive personal experience with an openly gay or lesbian person. The presence of openly gay/lesbian staff members is a crucial component of any school program seeking to reduce bigotry and provide support for lesbian and gay students. However, the vast majority of youth attend schools with no openly gay or lesbian personnel." [Governor's Commission on Gay and Lesbian Youth. (1993, February 25). *Making schools safe for gay and lesbian youth: Breaking the silence in schools and in families.* Publication #17296-60-500-2/93-C.R. Boston, MA: State House.]

Questions for Discussion

1. How do you feel about teachers "coming out" to their students?
2. Do you feel there should be gay teachers, coaches, etc., as role models for students?
3. If you support this concept, how can you present this to parents in order to elicit their support and acceptance?

Reading 4

"A wonderful child, with an incredible mind is gone because our society can't accept people who are 'different' from the norm. What an awful waste. I will miss my daughter for the rest of my life. I'll never see her beautiful smile or hear her glorious laugh. I'll never see her play with her sister again. All because of hatred and ignorance. I strongly believe that the seeds of hate are sown early in life. Let's replace them with love, understanding, and compassion. We have no choice. This terrible tragedy will continue to repeat itself and someday it may be your wonderful child who is gone forever." (Ruth, mother of a lesbian daughter who committed suicide, testifying at the Massachusetts Governor's Commission on Gay and Lesbian Youth, 1992)

Questions for Discussion

1. How do you feel about Ruth's story?
2. What advice would you offer Ruth?
3. What can be done to eliminate hatred and bigotry?
4. Identify steps you can take to eliminate prejudice in yourself and in the people with whom you interact?

Handout 4.5.   Permission is granted to photocopy for classroom use.

Activity 4.6
EFFECTS OF HOMOPHOBIA EXPERIENCED
BY GAY AND LESBIAN STUDENTS

Objective: To create an awareness and sensitivity among participants regarding the effects of homophobia in the educational system experienced by gay and lesbian students
Estimated Time: 45 to 50 minutes
Materials Needed: Easel, chart paper, and markers

Directions for Facilitators

1. Elicit answers and lead an open discussion on the following questions: How does homophobia affect gay and lesbian students and how do their responses develop? What are some examples?
2. List participant responses on chart paper. Make sure all of the responses listed below are included:

- isolation and loneliness,
- low self-esteem,
- suicide and suicide attempts,
- drug/alcohol abuse,
- low academic achievement,
- nonparticipation in school activities,
- fighting,
- dropping out of school,
- self-hatred,
- inability to participate in academic classes,
- fear,
- feelings of guilt,
- feel like an "outsider,"
- irresponsible sexual activity,
- victims of verbal and physical abuse,
- alienation from family, and
- homelessness.

Note: This activity may be followed by a videotape or audiotape featuring gay and lesbian teenagers expressing their views about how homophobia has affected them. Refer to Section XII for a list of supportive materials. (Workshop participants' discussion should follow.)

Activity 4.7
READINGS AND DISCUSSION

Objective: To provide supportive information regarding the workshop content through anecdotes, articles from the press, and testimonials
Estimated Time: 25 to 30 minutes
Materials Needed: Handout 4.7: Readings on Homophobia (4 copies)

Directions for Facilitators

1. Distribute the copies of Handout 4.7 to four volunteer participants. Assign one reading to each volunteer.
2. Ask them to read the selections to the entire group.
3. Facilitators should encourage discussion after each reading.

Key Points for Facilitators to Elicit

1. Educators need to be aware of the diversity of their student populations and be responsive to their needs.
2. Programs need to be developed for students, parents, and educators to enhance sensitivity to differences.

Handout 4.7
READINGS ON HOMOPHOBIA

Directions for Participants

1. Read aloud the assigned reading from below.
2. Help the facilitator lead a discussion on your reading using the suggested questions.

Reading 1

"When I was in eighth grade I saw three guys teasing a girl they heard was a lesbian. It happened behind the cafeteria building during the lunch period. They called her a dyke, threw her books in the cafeteria dumpster, and while two of the guys held her, the third one wrote 'DYKE' on her forehead with a magic marker. She was crying and ran off the school grounds. The guys saw me and threatened to beat me up if I told on them. I didn't report it at school, but I told my father and he told me to mind my own business. I don't know what happened after that; she looked like a regular girl to me." (Reported by a high school junior)

Questions for Discussion

1. How do you feel about this incident?
2. Do you feel the high school junior acted appropriately? How should he or she have responded?
3. Was Dad right in his advice to "mind my own business"?
4. How do you feel the guys should be dealt with? What disciplinary actions should the school take against them?
5. What suggestions would you have for handling this situation?

6. How can schools prevent this from happening? What curriculum changes or school policies could minimize the likelihood of these incidents?

Reading 2

"I felt different all the way through elementary school. When I got into middle school I knew what the difference was. I wasn't interested in girls and I hated listening to the guys talk about them, saying stuff that I knew was wrong; it was sickening. At first I tried to join them and pretend I was like them, but after awhile I couldn't do it anymore, so I stayed by myself and had no friends, boys or girls. I was called a 'faggot' and a 'queer' and worse than that. After school I went to my job and then went home. My parents helped me buy a car last summer and the second week after school started this year, someone broke into my car in the parking lot, stole my radio, slashed my two front tires, and left a sign in my car that said 'DIE FAG-GOT.' I couldn't do anything about it because it could have made my life worse. I can't wait until the end of this year, so I can get the hell out of here." (A high school senior's testimonial in a support group)

Questions for Discussion

1. What could have been done to help this student?
2. Should he have reported these incidents, and, if so, to whom?
3. How could an incident like this have been prevented?

Reading 3

"People don't know what it's like to have to hide your real self and be on guard all the time. I knew I was gay when I was 14 years old, but I lived a lie all the way through high school and my freshman year of college; I pretended to be like all the other guys. I dated, talked about conquests, hung out in bars, played sports—I did all the things straight guys do, but I was miserable. At the end of my freshman year my grades were so bad I quit before they threw me out. I went back to live with my parents and one night I was really depressed, had too much to drink, and swallowed a whole bottle of my mom's tranquilizers. I guess I'm one of the lucky ones; my Dad found me, called 911, and they saved my life. Since I've been in this support group my life has turned around and I'm going back to college to start over." (Testimonial in a support group)

Questions for Discussion

1. What warning signs did this student send?
2. What could have been done to recognize he was hurting?
3. How could the school system have been of assistance?
4. What could have helped this student feel better about himself?

Reading 4

"It is the duty of school administrators to provide a safe environment for all students and when they do not protect gay and lesbian students from physical or verbal harassment, they are not fulfilling their duty. The source of an administrator's responsibility to ensure a safe environment for all students is the compulsory education law. The students are legally entrusted to the care of school officials and if they do not take action when gay and lesbian students are verbally or physically harassed, they are neglecting their lawful duty." [Dennis, D., & Harlow, R. E.

(1986). Gay youth and the right to education. *Yale Law & Policy Review, 4*(2), 451.]

Questions for Discussion

1. How do you feel about this reading?
2. If you support the presented views, how can this best be implemented in school systems?
3. Should gay and lesbian students attend separate schools such as the Harvey Milk School?

Handout 4.7.   Permission is granted to photocopy for classroom use.

Activity 4.8
EDUCATING TO REDUCE AND PREVENT
HOMOPHOBIA

Objective: To encourage participants to be proactive in their schools to reduce and prevent homophobia
Estimated Time: 45 to 50 minutes
Materials Needed: Chart paper and markers for participants; masking tape

Directions for Facilitators

1. Organize participants into groups of six.
2. Ask each group to establish and chart a list of specific actions they think could and should be taken in schools and colleges to reduce and prevent homophobia and how these activities can be implemented. Each group should select a leader who will post the chart and report to the full group of participants.
3. Facilitators should encourage discussion as each group presents. If the charts do not reflect the following list of possible actions, facilitators should fill in the gaps:

Institute curriculum innovations that educate all students about homophobia and its effects. (Suggested curriculum areas: social sciences, language arts, business courses that focus on the workplace, health courses, peer counseling, American history, government, fine arts, etc.)

Provide inservice workshops for faculties, administrators, school psychologists, guidance personnel, school district social workers, curriculum directors, media specialists, school nurses, visiting teachers, school board members, undergraduate and graduate college professors and instructors, human resource development personnel, and noninstructional personnel who deal with students.

Enlist the help of local professional organizations to promote policies to protect the rights of gay and lesbian students and teachers and to provide a safe learning environment.

Adopt school policies protecting gay and lesbian students and teachers from harassment, discrimination, and violence.

Include gay and lesbian issues within appropriate policies and programs concerning diversity or multiculturalism.

Promote changes in teacher-training programs and teacher certification standards that require teachers, counselors, and other educators to receive training in issues relevant to the needs of gay and lesbian students.

Initiate school-based support groups open to all students, including self-identified gay and lesbian youth, heterosexual students supportive of their gay and lesbian peers, and any students wishing to discuss gay and lesbian issues in a safe and confidential environment. Faculty advisors should be appointed to sponsor these groups and serve as a liaison to administrators, communicating group needs.

Provide specific training for school counselors to prepare them to support gay and lesbian youth and make appropriate resources and other information available to students and their families.

Provide print and nonprint information in school media centers on gay and lesbian issues for the use of student populations.

Break the silence that exists in most educational institutions.

Key Points for Facilitators to Elicit

1. Many actions can be implemented to reduce and prevent homophobia.
2. Silence encourages and helps perpetuate homophobia.

Activity 4.9
BELIEFS CONCERNING GAYS AND LESBIANS

Objective: To promote the examination of participants' beliefs about gays and lesbians

Estimated Time: 30 to 40 minutes

Materials Needed: Handout 4.9 (Part A): Beliefs Concerning Gays and Lesbians (one copy for each participant), Handout 4.9 (Part B): Group Composite Tallies (one for each table of six participants)

Directions for Facilitators

1. Organize participants into groups of six.
2. Distribute one copy of Handout 4.9 (Part A) to each participant and ask them to follow the instructions. (Allow 5 minutes for this activity.)
3. After participants complete the individual handout, distribute one copy of Handout 4.9 (Part B) to each table and ask participants to follow the instructions. (Allow 5 minutes for this activity.)
4. As each table leader reports the majority tallies for each statement to the total workshop group, encourage discussion on the statements.

Questions for Discussion

1. Why do you feel there are such strong beliefs about this statement?
2. Why and how do you think these beliefs have developed?
3. Do these statements help promote or dissuade homophobic thinking?
4. Should steps be taken to modify this belief? If yes, what steps can be taken?

Key Points for Facilitators to Elicit

1. There may be strong opinions about gays and lesbians.
2. Education is an avenue for addressing and possibly modifying diverging opinions.

Handout 4.9 (Part A)
BELIEFS CONCERNING GAYS AND LESBIANS

Directions for Participants

Indicate your level of agreement with each statement by placing a check in the appropriate space. Respond with your initial reaction. (You will have 5 minutes to complete this activity.)

D = Disagree; PD = Unsure, Probably Disagree; PA = Unsure, Probably Agree; A = Agree

		D	PD	PA	A
1.	Being gay/lesbian is a choice.	—	—	—	—
2.	Gays/lesbians should have the legal right to adopt children.	—	—	—	—
3.	Most child molesters are gays and lesbians.	—	—	—	—
4.	People who have strong homophobic beliefs tend to be religious and frequent churchgoers.	—	—	—	—
5.	Gays and lesbians should try to be heterosexual.	—	—	—	—
6.	Public schools should teach about gay and lesbian orientations in sex education classes.	—	—	—	—
7.	American high schools should have gay and lesbian support groups.	—	—	—	—
8.	American public schools should outlaw discrimination against gay and lesbian students.	—	—	—	—
9.	Gays and lesbians should not become ordained religious leaders.	—	—	—	—

	D	PD	PA	A
10. Gays and lesbians should not be hired for high-security government positions.	—	—	—	—
11. Gay and lesbian domestic partners should receive workplace benefits.	—	—	—	—

Handout 4.9 (Part A).   Permission is granted to photocopy for classroom use.

Handout 4.9 (Part B)
BELIEFS CONCERNING GAYS AND LESBIANS
GROUP TALLY

Directions for Participants

1. Select someone from your group to record the number of each type of response to each statement from the individual group members. For example, for statement #1, the totals might look like this:

D	PD	PA	A
2	1	0	3

2. Discuss briefly within your group those statements for which there seems to be the most consensus and those for which opinions appear to differ strongly (for example, three group members marked "D" and three marked "A"). (Please remember to be respectful of other participants' opinions.)

3. As the tallies are shared with all workshop participants, assist the facilitator in a discussion of the tallies and why each statement was marked as it was.

D = Disagree; PD = Unsure, Probably Disagree; PA = Unsure, Probably Agree; A = Agree

	D	PD	PA	A
1. Being gay/lesbian is a choice.	___	___	___	___
2. Gays/lesbians should have the legal right to adopt children.	___	___	___	___
3. Most child molesters are gays and lesbians.	___	___	___	___
4. People who have strong homophobic beliefs tend to be religious and frequent churchgoers.	___	___	___	___
5. Gays and lesbians should try to be heterosexual.	___	___	___	___

	D	PD	PA	A
6. Public schools should teach about gay and lesbian orientations in sex education classes.	—	—	—	—
7. American high schools should have gay and lesbian support groups.	—	—	—	—
8. American public schools should outlaw discrimination against gay and lesbian students.	—	—	—	—
9. Gays and lesbians should not become ordained religious leaders.	—	—	—	—
10. Gays and lesbians should not be hired for high-security government positions.	—	—	—	—
11. Gay and lesbian domestic partners should receive workplace benefits.	—	—	—	—
Total tallies:	—	—	—	—

Handout 4.9 (Part B).   Permission is granted to photocopy for classroom use.

Activity 4.10
CONSEQUENCES OF ACTIONS RELATIVE
TO GAYS AND LESBIANS

Objective: To focus on the effect of particular actions involving gays and lesbians and promote relevant discussion among participants

Estimated Time: 55 to 60 minutes

Materials Needed: Handout 4.10: Consequences of Actions Relative to Gays and Lesbians (one copy for each group)

Directions for Facilitators

1. Organize groups of four or five participants each.
2. Distribute Handout 4.10 (one to each group) and ask participants to follow the instructions. (Allow approximately 45 minutes for individual groups to discuss the actions and complete the chart.)
3. When groups have completed the chart, initiate discussion by calling on each group to report its decisions and see if group consensus is possible.

Key Points for Facilitators to Elicit

1. Every action, no matter how innocent, can have a negative impact on others.
2. Individuals need to be sensitive to their actions and feelings.
3. Humor can at times be offensive.

Handout 4.10
CONSEQUENCES OF ACTIONS RELATIVE
TO GAYS AND LESBIANS

Directions for Participants

1. Discuss with your group members each of the six actions listed below.
2. Record possible positive and/or negative consequences for each item. (You will have approximately 45 minutes for this activity.)
3. As called upon by the facilitator, share your group's comments with all workshop participants.

Action	Positive Consequences	Negative Consequences
1. Not laughing at a derogatory joke involving gays/ lesbians.		
2. Reporting a discriminatory incident to a superior.		

3. Laughing at a
   derogatory joke
   involving gays/
   lesbians.

   _____ _____
   _____ _____
   _____ _____
   _____ _____
   _____ _____
   _____ _____
   _____ _____

4. Ignoring a child's
   derogatory
   name-calling
   re: gays/lesbians.

   _____ _____
   _____ _____
   _____ _____
   _____ _____
   _____ _____
   _____ _____

5. Ignoring verbal
   harassment of a
   gay/lesbian couple.

   _____ _____
   _____ _____
   _____ _____
   _____ _____
   _____ _____

6. Making a
   derogatory
   comment or telling
   a joke about
   gays/lesbians.

   _____ _____
   _____ _____
   _____ _____
   _____ _____
   _____ _____
   _____ _____

Handout 4.10.   Permission is granted to photocopy for classroom use.

IDENTIFYING AND ASSISTING YOUTH IN NEED

Most young people who have a sexual orientation that is different from the accepted norm find it difficult to live comfortably in a society where homophobia is rampant. They have many survival decisions to make, the most frequent of which is to hide their sexual orientation from everyone. This single decision may impose a great psychological burden and create a multitude of related problems.

The fact that children in our society are required by law to attend school until they are sixteen years of age means educators are in a position to provide assistance to adolescents who are struggling with a different sexual orientation. Because most of these young people seem no different from their heterosexual peers, their uniqueness eludes even the most perceptive of educators. Pretending to be someone they are not, and the constant emotional turmoil, can place these students at risk for academic failure, depression, alcohol/drug abuse, suicide, sexually transmitted diseases, teenage pregnancies, etc., as they try to cope with fear, isolation, and guilt.

This section is intended to stimulate thought and dialogue among workshop participants about how these students in need may be identified and assisted. Activity 5.1: Brainstorming At-Risk Behavioral Indicators is designed to culminate in a list of some at-risk behaviors that may be connected to sexual orientation confusion. Activity 5.2: Case Study: Aaron Fricke illustrates one of the ways an openly gay high school student coped with his sexual orientation within an atmosphere of homophobia. Activity 5.3: Providing Assistance for Youth with Diverse Sexual Orientations stimulates participants to think of ways help can be provided in our secondary schools and colleges for students in need, particularly those who have been driven by fear to remain "invisible."

Activity 5.1
BRAINSTORMING AT-RISK BEHAVIORAL INDICATORS

Objective: To stimulate dialogue concerning the signals gay and lesbian youth send to professionals who work with them in schools and colleges
Materials Needed: Chart pad and markers for facilitators; pencils and paper for participants
Estimated Time: 40 to 45 minutes

Directions for Facilitators

1. Organize participants into groups of four.
2. Review the Background Information with participants, *with the exception of the list of at-risk behavioral indicators*.
3. Ask each group to brainstorm the following question and compile a list of at-risk behavioral indicators to be contributed to a master list: "What are some behavioral indicators that may signify that a student is at-risk due to confusion related to his or her sexual orientation?" (Allow 20 minutes for this part of the activity.)
4. After the allotted time, ask one participant from each group to read the list from his or her group.
5. Chart the indicators, avoiding duplication. (Compare the list of indicators from the Background Information with those on the master list. Add those that do not already appear on the master list.)
6. Hold an open discussion using the questions provided.

Questions for Discussion

1. In your current role as a professional or citizen, what courses of action might you take if a young gay or lesbian chose you as a confidant?
2. Consider ways:

    to establish and maintain confidentiality and trust,
    to offer available referrals within the educational system, community, or
       workplace, and/or
    to provide appropriate information services.

Key Points for Facilitators to Elicit

1. Students will send signals to others that indicate they are "at risk."
2. Educators need to be aware of the indicators of "at-risk" behaviors and know how to respond to their students.
3. Some at-risk students may exhibit only one at-risk behavioral indicator. One indicator alone is worthy of further investigation.

BACKGROUND INFORMATION

Throughout the literature, gay and lesbian youth are referred to as "the invisible," "the silent minority," "youth with hidden lives," or "closeted sons and daughters." Despite the "coming out" movement of today's gay and lesbian teenagers and the growing support of parents and educational organizations, the large majority of gay and lesbian teenagers and young adults is still invisible, silent, closeted, and isolated.

Homophobia continues to haunt young gays and lesbians, putting many of them at risk for suicide, alcoholism, substance abuse, dropping out of school, running away from home, academic failure, lowered self-esteem, and poor peer relationships. So long as sexual diversity is ignored or misunderstood, and heterosexist attitudes prevail, gays and lesbians will continue to suffer. A large majority of gay and lesbian young people have learned through fear that their safety depends on their silence and nondisclosure. This section is designed to help professionals realize that approximately 10% of our youth are gay or lesbian— representing all religious, ethnic, racial, and socioeconomic backgrounds—and that education and professional leadership is needed to provide help for the gays and lesbians in our schools, colleges, and the workplace. Gays and lesbians come to terms with their sexuality at different ages; many report they knew they were "different" in childhood, whereas others may not become aware of their sexual orientation until the adult years. Most seem to become aware during adolescence and young adulthood. Gay and lesbian youth spend their childhoods, preteen, and teenage years in a heterosexual world and learn what is expected of them from the significant people in their lives (parents, siblings, peers, relatives, the clergy, and teachers). Television, movies, books, magazines, music, and other media reinforce these expectations. These young people learn about family, friendships, how to make themselves attractive to the opposite sex, dating, and romantic love between males and females.

Homophobic attitudes can become a subtle influence as early as the preschool years and become more and more influential as children attend school and begin to hear derogatory terms relating to homosexuality used by their peers. They may not understand these derogatory expressions, but they quickly learn that anyone attracted to his or her own sex is considered "bad," "a freak," and unacceptable by society. Adult role models often reinforce homophobic attitudes in various ways, which may result in forcing young gays and lesbians into the "closet." Unable to fulfill expectations and threatened by society's homophobic attitudes, young gays and lesbians may become fearful, isolated, guilt ridden, depressed, and unable to establish direction in their lives.

Many gays and lesbians search for confidants with whom they may safely discuss their awareness of their same-sex interests. This search is usually for an adult who is perceived to be kind, accepting, sympathetic, and trustworthy. Frequently these confidants are chosen from the professionals who are part of the daily lives of young gays and lesbians, such as teachers, members of the clergy, coaches, guidance counselors, or physicians. Fear, or lack of courage, may prevent young gays and lesbians from being open in their expression of their feelings. Fortunately, there are behavioral indicators that may warn professionals that these young people are at risk. These signals should not be ignored.

Background Information for Activity 5.1.   Permission is granted to photocopy for classroom use.

(*Note*: Do not reveal the following information to participants until Activity 5.1 has been completed. If you have decided to use the Background Information as a handout, remember to cover this portion when making copies.) Below are some at-risk behavioral indicators:

- poor self-image,
- low self-esteem,
- social isolation,
- hostility toward authority,
- underachievement,
- immature behavior,
- failure to establish goals,
- rebellion,
- negative attitudes,
- depression,
- aggression toward peers,
- running away from home,
- truancy from school,
- alcohol and drug abuse,
- unusual emotional attachments to specific adults,
- unusual shyness,
- inability to concentrate, and/or
- suicide attempts.

Activity 5.2
CASE STUDY: AARON FRICKE

Objective: To encourage thought and dialogue among participants and to help them examine their attitudes regarding diverse sexual orientations

Estimated Time: 35 to 40 minutes

Materials Needed: Handout 5.2: Case Study: Aaron Fricke (one copy for each group)

Directions for Facilitators

1. Organize participants in groups of five or six.
2. Distribute one copy of Handout 5.2 to each group and ask them to follow the directions listed on the handout. (Allow 20 to 25 minutes for the small group activity.)
3. After the allotted time limit, have each group leader report the consensus on each of the four questions.
4. After all reports have been completed, the workshop facilitators should encourage open discussion regarding the substance of the activity.

Questions for Discussion

1. Should all students be able to bring whatever guest they wish to school-sponsored activities?
2. Should there be school-based policies or legislation protecting gay and lesbian rights?
3. Can the entire group arrive at a consensus on these issues?

Handout 5.2
CASE STUDY: AARON FRICKE

Directions for Participants

1. Choose a leader from the group to facilitate the activity.
2. The group leader reads the case study aloud to the group.
3. The group leader poses the four questions that follow and tries to lead the group to a consensus for each question.
4. Record the answers on the handout. (You should spend approximately 20 to 25 minutes to complete steps 1 through 4.)
5. Report the results to the entire group of workshop participants. (If consensus is impossible, the leader should report the reasons.)

In 1980 a gay high school student in Cumberland, Rhode Island, made the decision to invite a male date to the senior prom. He wanted to make "a statement" about his sexual orientation and his human rights. After meeting with opposition from the administration, he sued the school for the right to take his same-sex date to the dance. The judge ruled in Fricke's favor and he was allowed to attend the prom with his male date. (*Note*: Although other cities, such as Boston and Detroit, have held dances for gay and lesbian students, on May 20, 1994, the Los Angeles Unified School District became the first school district in the nation to sponsor a gay and lesbian junior–senior prom. The dance was held at the Hilton Hotel in downtown Los Angeles. There were more than 100 couples in attendance.)

Questions for Discussion

1. Did Fricke make the right decision to take his same-sex date to the prom? *Why or why not?*
   Consensus: _____

   _____

_____

_____

_____

2. Did the principal make the right decision to ban Fricke and his date from attending the prom? *Why or why not?*
    Consensus: _____

    _____

    _____

    _____

    _____

3. Was Fricke right in filing a lawsuit against the school? *Why or why not?*
    Consensus: _____

    _____

    _____

    _____

    _____

4. Did the judge who adjudicated the case make the right decision? *Why or why not?*
    Consensus: _____

    _____

    _____

    _____

    _____

Handout 5.2.   Permission is granted to photocopy for classroom use.

Activity 5.3
PROVIDING ASSISTANCE FOR YOUTH WITH DIVERSE SEXUAL ORIENTATIONS

Objective: To create an awareness among participants of actions that may be taken by professionals to assist gay and lesbian youth in middle school, high school, and college settings
Estimated Time: 40 to 45 minutes
Materials Needed: Handout 5.3: Assisting Youth in Need (two copies for each group)

Directions for Facilitators

1. Organize participants into groups of four and ask them to work in pairs.
2. Distribute two copies of Handout 5.3 to each group. Ask them to follow the directions on the handout. (Remind them of the time constraints noted in the directions and call time after the first 15 minutes to remind them to move on to Step 3 of their instructions.)
3. After both activities on the handout have been completed, call upon a few randomly selected pairs to read their lists to all workshop participants. Encourage discussion as the lists are shared.
4. If the participants' lists do not address the following suggestions, chart those that were not addressed and discuss them with participants.

- integrate the following topics in appropriate curricula: homophobia, pluralism, human relations, and diversity
- provide student access to accurate information regarding diverse sexual orientations
- support sex education that includes information about the risks related to HIV/AIDS and sexually transmitted diseases
- provide information to students concerning the educational and community referral networks
- encourage school-based support groups for gay and lesbian students and their families
- stress the importance of maintaining student trust and confidentiality
- promote policies that provide for a safe environment for all students
- emphasize to educators the importance of being nonjudgmental concerning diverse sexual orientations
- suggest or initiate school programs that break the silence concerning diverse sexual orientations

- provide counseling services that include the needs of students with diverse sexual orientations
- address attitudes concerning diverse sexual orientations in curricula that deal with multiculturalism, attitudes, beliefs, and values
- include gay and lesbian issues in social studies classes that deal with civil rights, the Constitution, political activism, public opinion, the judicial system, pressure groups, legislation, states' rights, presidential powers, the military, prejudice, and discrimination
- include training for all educators (elementary, secondary, and college) on suicide prevention, dropout prevention, and the prevention of violence
- mention, in appropriate classes, the issues of gays and lesbians in biographical studies of literary figures, scientists, inventors, artists, musicians, political leaders, composers, entertainers, mathematicians, sports champions, actors, entrepreneurs, and other renowned contributors who may serve as role models for gay and lesbian students

Handout 5.3
ASSISTING YOUTH IN NEED

Directions for Participants

1. With your partner, select one of the three educational settings and one professional listed under the educational setting you selected.
2. Brainstorm with your partner and make a list of what the professional could do to help students of diverse sexual orientations. (You will have 15 minutes of working time.)
3. After time has been called by the facilitators, both pairs of each group should share and discuss the two lists within the small group for 10 minutes.
4. Be prepared to read your list aloud to all workshop participants and participate in the large group discussion.

Middle School	High School	College
Principal	Guidance director	Counselor
Social studies	Principal	Administrator
teacher	Health education	or Dean
Media specialist	teacher	Literature
Health education	Social studies	instructor
teacher	teacher	Sociology
School		instructor
nurse	English	Director of
Physical	teacher	student
education	School	affairs
teacher	psychologist	Head
Guidance	Media	librarian
director	specialist	Resident
		assistant

Record the educational setting selected:_____
Record the professional selected: _____
List what the professional could do in his or her position
to help students of diverse sexual orientations:

1. _____

   _____

   _____

2. _____

   _____

   _____

3. _____

   _____

   _____

4. _____

   _____

   _____

5. _____

   _____

   _____

6. _____

   _____

   _____

7. _____

   _____

   _____

8. _____

   _____

   _____

9. _____

_____

_____

10. _____

_____

_____

_____

Handout 5.3.   Permission is granted to photocopy for classroom use.

EDUCATIONAL AND WORKPLACE ISSUES AND PROGRAMS TO PROMOTE POSITIVE CHANGE

A few local and state governments in the United States have passed legislation to protect employees from discrimination on the basis of sexual orientation, but, to date, there is no federal legislation. Many employers have voluntarily adopted policies of nondiscrimination, especially large corporations. Major businesses, such as AT&T, Levi Strauss, E.I. duPont de Nemours, Sun Microsystems, and Apple Computer are serving as examples for their corporate counterparts.

In 1994, the Commonwealth of Massachusetts adopted the nation's first educational policy prohibiting discrimination against gay and lesbian elementary and secondary students and teachers. The policy provides for a variety of programs that are contributing to positive changes in the Massachusetts schools. A few other states and local school systems are at various stages in the development of policy plans to protect gay and lesbian students and teachers from discrimination.

There are numerous gay and lesbian issues in the workplace and educational settings that require resolution, if gays and lesbians are to exercise their equal rights. Activity 6.1: Identifying Issues in the Workplace gives participants the opportunity to discuss gay and lesbian issues in the workplace and consider suggestions for positive change. Activity 6.2: Case Studies: Jane Doe, Joyce, Jim, and Mr. Russell is meant to elicit discussion of on-the-job cases to familiarize participants with real issues faced by gay and lesbian employees. Activity 6.3: What Would You Do? presents three workplace and school scenarios for participants' discussion and response. Activity 6.4: Problems and Solutions Associated with Gays and Lesbians in Educational and Workplace Settings is designed to stimulate participants to identify problems gays and lesbians experience in workplace and educational settings and to think seriously about solutions. Activity 6.5: Promoting Positive Attitudes at School and in the Workplace culminates in some specific suggestions for helping to change attitudes in schools and in the workplace.

Activity 6.1
IDENTIFYING ISSUES IN THE WORKPLACE

Objective: To help participants identify and respond to issues in the workplace that relate to employees with a diverse sexual orientation

Estimated Time: 55 to 60 minutes

Materials Needed: Chart pad, easel, and markers for facilitators; paper and pencil for each group; Handout 6.1: Gay and Lesbian Issues in the Workplace and Suggestions for Positive Change (one copy for each group)

Directions for Facilitators

1. Organize participants into groups of four or five.
2. Present the Background Information to participants.
3. Distribute Handout 6.1 (one copy to each group) and ask them to follow the instructions. (Estimated time for completing this part of the activity: 20 to 25 minutes.)
4. After the allotted time, ask a representative from each group to share the group's suggestions. Chart at least two or three suggestions from each group.
5. After all groups have contributed their suggestions, compare them with the information from #2 of the Key Points provided below.

Questions for Discussion

1. How can gay and lesbian activists influence federal legislation to prevent job discrimination on the basis of sexual orientation?
2. What specific actions can employers take to pressure insurance carriers to provide benefits for gay and lesbian employees?
3. What specific actions can gay and lesbian employees take to eliminate the "glass ceiling"?

Key Points for Facilitators to Elicit

1. The majority of American workplaces are not "gay friendly." As a result, gay and lesbian employees have learned to hide their sexual orientation, causing numerous problems.

2. Some suggestions for making positive changes in the workplace are as follows:

    a. making discrimination based on sexual orientation as impermissible as discrimination because of race, nationality, age, or gender
    b. organizing gays and lesbians in the workplace to negotiate with employers for bereavement leave and leave to care for a sick same-gender domestic partner
    c. top management showing support for gay and lesbian employees, to set an example in the workplace
    d. employers adopting written nondiscrimination policies, making them public, and enforcing them within the workplace
    e. making it known to all employees that providing a safe and comfortable environment for all employees is a top management priority
    f. encouraging gay and lesbian employees to take an active part in educating nongay employees about gay and lesbian issues and concerns
    g. lobbying for benefits afforded married heterosexual employees (e.g., medical, dental)
    h. promoting diversity training for all employees to encourage tolerance, reduce homophobia, and provide accurate information regarding diverse sexual orientations
    i. making it known to all employees that it is safe for gay and lesbian employees to become "visible" in the workplace

BACKGROUND INFORMATION

Professionals in education and other types of workplaces should be aware that their colleagues or employees may be of diverse sexual orientations and that some may be closeted and some may not. Others may seem to be heterosexual, because they are divorced, married, or date the opposite sex. In any case, people are usually hired because of their merit and work qualifications, and usually they are assumed to be heterosexual.

People are most productive when they feel comfortable in their environment and do not have to hide who they really are. It is debilitating to have to pretend to be someone that one is not, and often the energy wasted on pretense reduces employee creativity and productivity.

Antidiscrimination policies regarding sexual orientation have been established and made public by numerous employers throughout the nation, including such large corporations as AT&T, Apple Computer, Levi Strauss, and Allstate Insurance. These stated policies allow employees of diverse sexual orientations to feel safe and comfortable in the workplace, to avoid pretense, and to be fully productive in their jobs.

Employers or administrators who assume all employees or students are heterosexual and who tolerate homophobic attitudes in the workplace or educational setting promote dishonesty, guilt, fear, anxiety, and pretense among their employees or students with diverse sexual orientations.

Background Information for Activity 6.1.   Permission is granted to photocopy for classroom use.

Handout 6.1
GAY AND LESBIAN ISSUES IN THE WORKPLACE
AND SUGGESTIONS FOR POSITIVE CHANGE

Directions for Participants

1. The material below concerning gay and lesbian issues in the workplace was compiled by gay and lesbian activists. Read through the list and discuss the issues within your group.
2. As a group, come up with at least five general suggestions for achieving positive change in the workplace. Be prepared to share your suggestions with all the workshop participants. (You will have 20 to 25 minutes to complete this activity.)

Gay and Lesbian Issues in the Workplace

1. The need for same-gender domestic partner benefits (e.g., medical, dental, pensions)
2. The need for leave time to care for a sick same-gender domestic partner as well as bereavement leave for the death of a same-gender domestic partner
3. Working in an environment of overt homophobia
4. Establishing freedom for gay and lesbian employees to be "visible" in the workplace without retaliation
5. Welcoming of same-gender domestic partners at workplace social events whenever husbands and wives are invited
6. Breaking the "glass ceiling" beyond which gays and lesbians find difficulty being promoted to middle and upper management positions and boards of directors
7. Job discrimination based on sexual orientation

Handout 6.1.   Permission is granted to photocopy for classroom use.

Activity 6.2
CASE STUDIES: JANE DOE, JOYCE, JIM, AND MR. RUSSELL

Objective: To encourage thought and dialogue among participants that will help them examine their attitudes regarding diverse sexual orientations

Estimated Time: 55 to 60 minutes

Materials Needed: Handout 6.2 (Part A): Case Study: Jane Doe; Handout 6.2 (Part B): Case Study: Joyce; Handout 6.2 (Part C): Case Study: Jim; and Handout 6.2 (Part D): Case Study: Mr. Russell (one copy of each for each group)

Directions for Facilitators

1. Organize participants in groups of five or six.
2. Distribute one copy of Handout 6.2 (Part A), Handout 6.2 (Part B), Handout 6.2 (Part C), and Handout 6.2 (Part D) to each group and ask them to follow the directions listed on the handouts. (Allow 30 to 35 minutes for this small group activity.)
3. After the allotted time, have each group leader report the group consensus on each question of the case studies.
4. After all reports have been completed, the facilitators should encourage open discussion.

Questions for Discussion

1. Should there be workplace policies regarding harassment or discrimination based on sexual orientation?
2. Should gays and lesbians be encouraged to be open regarding their sexual orientation at work?
3. What types of sexual orientation disclosure are acceptable at work for heterosexuals? Gays and lesbians?
4. Do you feel these case studies are representative of common real-life situations? How frequently do you think such things occur?

Key Points for Facilitators to Elicit

1. Most employees want to feel they are employed based on their qualifications and merit.

2. Every large workplace or educational setting is apt to have a diverse range of sexual orientations.
3. Numerous public and private employers are adopting antidiscrimination policies for employees.

Handout 6.2 (Part A)
CASE STUDY: JANE DOE

Directions for Participants

1. Choose a leader from your group to facilitate the activity.
2. Listen as your group leader reads the case study aloud to the group.
3. Read the four questions at the end of the case study. Try to reach a consensus within your group and then record the answers on the handout.
4. Your group leader will be called on to report the results to the entire group of workshop participants. (If consensus is impossible, the leader should report the reasons.)

Jane Doe was a closeted lesbian, employed for eight years as a branch manager for a nationwide banking firm. She was told she had been selected for a promotion to regional manager. Two days before her appointment, the bank president received an anonymous note informing him of Jane's sexual orientation. When confronted with the allegation by the bank president, who said he was not at liberty to reveal the information source, Jane admitted her sexual orientation. The next day he informed her that he had been instructed, through a conference call with the national banking executive, to let her know her regional appointment had been retracted and if she chose to remain as an employee, she would be demoted to the position of teller.

Jane consulted an attorney and was told there is no federal law that prevents private employers from undercompensating, demoting, firing, or refusing to hire a gay or lesbian employee solely because of that person's sexual orientation, regardless of aptitude or work record. Furthermore, she was employed in a city and state that did not forbid discrimination based on sexual orientation. The attorney discouraged her from taking any legal action.

1. Did Jane make the right decision in admitting her
    sexual orientation. *Why or why not?*

    _____

    _____

    _____

2. Was the bank executive right in retracting the
    regional managership? *Why or why not?*

    _____

    _____

    _____

3. Should there be a federal law prohibiting private
    employers from discriminating against a gay or les-
    bian employee solely because of that person's sexual
    orientation? *Why or why not?*

    _____

    _____

    _____

4. What could Jane do to reconstruct her career and
    what role might the bank president play?

    _____

    _____

    _____

Handout 6.2 (Part A).   Permission is granted to photocopy for classroom use.

Handout 6.2 (Part B)
CASE STUDY: JOYCE

Directions for Participants

1. Choose a leader from your group to facilitate the activity.
2. Listen as your group leader reads the case study aloud to the group.
3. Read the four questions at the end of the case study. Try to reach a consensus within your group and then record the answers on the handout.
4. Your group leader will be called on to report the results to the entire group of workshop participants. (If consensus is impossible, the leader should report the reasons.)

Joyce has worked as a secretary in a New York City accounting firm for two years, since her graduation from high school. She is a lesbian and has lived with her domestic partner since they both moved to New York from a small Connecticut town. Both of them are closeted at work. With both their salaries, they barely meet living expenses.

Six months after Joyce's employment began, the president of the firm, impressed by her intelligence, loyalty, and job performance, convinced her to enroll in college night classes, earn a degree in accounting, and become an accountant with the firm. After she agreed to follow the plan, the president used his influence with a bank to arrange for Joyce to take out a substantial loan to pay her college expenses. Thinking she had job security, Joyce did not anticipate any problem making the loan payments.

Joyce had no idea what the president's attitudes were concerning gays and lesbians and she wasn't concerned about it. Their conversations were always work related; he never asked her personal questions.

One day the president asked her if she would be willing to accept a dinner date with his favorite nephew who was visiting for the weekend. Because the nephew lived and worked in Los Angeles, which meant she would probably not have to see him again, and because she felt somewhat obligated to her boss, she accepted. It turned out the nephew was very attracted to Joyce and became sexually aggressive while they were riding in a taxi. When he discovered the attraction wasn't mutual, he became angry, they had an argument, and he accused her of being a "dyke." At the next traffic light, she got out of the cab and took the subway back to her apartment. The following Monday morning she was confronted by her boss, who seemed angry and asked if she were a "dyke."

1. Considering the circumstances, how should Joyce respond? Why?

_____

_____

_____

2. Do you feel her position is in jeopardy?

_____

_____

_____

3. Is there a way she can turn this situation into something positive? If yes, how? If no, why not?

_____

_____

_____

4. Should there be workplace policies regarding socialization with other employees or their families?

_____

_____

_____

Handout 6.2 (Part B).   Permission is granted to photocopy for classroom use.

Handout 6.2 (Part C)
CASE STUDY: JIM

Directions for Participants

1. Choose a leader from your group to facilitate the activity.
2. Listen as your group leader reads the case study aloud to the group.
3. Read the four questions at the end of the case study. Try to reach a consensus within your group and then record the answers on the handout.
4. Your group leader will be called on to report the results to the entire group of workshop participants. (If consensus is impossible, the leader should report the reasons.)

Jim is a 26-year-old closeted gay career police officer. He has been employed by an urban police department for five years. During his service he has been promoted twice and has received three commendations. His goal is to become a police lieutenant. Jim's captain is known to be antigay and condones open homophobic attitudes in the department. Protected by the anonymity of an urban environment, Jim has managed to remain closeted while living with his gay partner.

Jim has been assigned a new patrol partner who is a personal friend of the captain, has a deep hatred for homosexuals, and is obsessed about "hunting" and arresting gay men. When they have night patrol duty, the partner insists upon "hunting" gays, verbally and physically harassing them until they are forced to defend themselves, and arresting them for attacking an officer. Jim does not participate in his partner's modus operandi.

1. What should Jim do about this situation? Why?

_____

_____

_____

2. Can he handle this situation without revealing his sexual orientation? If yes, how?

_____

_____

_____

3. Are there actions that can be taken to prevent these incidents?

_____

_____

_____

Handout 6.2 (Part C).   Permission is granted to photocopy for classroom use.

Handout 6.2 (Part D)
CASE STUDY: MR. RUSSELL

Directions for Participants

1. Choose a leader from your group to facilitate the activity.
2. Listen as your group leader reads the case study aloud to the group.
3. Read the four questions at the end of the case study. Try to reach a consensus within your group and then record the answers on the handout.
4. Your group leader will be called on to report the results to the entire group of workshop participants. (If consensus is impossible, the leader should report the reasons.)

Mr. Russell, a first-year teacher, was recruited from his college campus to teach physical education in a suburban high school 1,600 miles away. By the time he established residency, the move had cost him about $2,000, which he borrowed from his parents. In addition to P.E., his teaching duties included one class of health education and being assistant coach for the junior varsity football team. He worked hard and was well liked by the students, faculty, and administration. His first-semester evaluation, written and signed by the principal, stated he was an excellent teacher and coach.

Donald, the quarterback for the football team, was also a student in Mr. Russell's health education class. Donald's parents were in the process of a difficult divorce and he confided in Mr. Russell concerning the decision he would have to make about whether to live with his mother or father. Mr. Russell and Donald had lengthy talks about this issue and as a result they became very friendly.

During the second semester, after Mr. Russell had taught the mandatory sex education unit in health education, Donald confided in Mr. Russell once again, admitting he was having a homosexual relationship with another student. He told Mr. Russell he was depressed, felt guilty, and was thinking of committing suicide. In his attempt to comfort Donald, Mr. Russell admitted, in confidence, that he also was gay. He recommended Donald talk with a school guidance counselor. Two days later, the principal called Mr. Russell to his office and informed him he was not being rehired for the next year because the administration would be looking for an experienced replacement. There was no discussion and Mr. Russell was dismissed from the principal's office.

1. What might have occurred during the time between Mr. Russell's last talk with Donald and his meeting with the principal?

_____

_____

_____

2. What did Mr. Russell do right or wrong?

_____

_____

_____

3. What do you think Mr. Russell should do?

_____

_____

_____

4. Are there any educational policies that may be involved in this case study? If yes, what are they?

_____

_____

_____

Activity 6.3
WHAT WOULD YOU DO?

Objective: To present several scenarios and have participants assess the difference between how they might feel versus act if faced with these dilemmas
Estimated Time: 25 to 30 minutes
Materials Needed: Handout 6.3: Scenarios (one copy for each participant)

Directions for Facilitators

1. Distribute one copy of Handout 6.3 to each participant.
2. Ask them to read each scenario and prepare to discuss their responses. (Allow 15 minutes for the completion of this exercise.)
3. Facilitate a group discussion using the questions provided.

Questions for Discussion

1. How comfortable were you with these scenarios?
2. What aspect of this assignment made you most uncomfortable?
3. Is there a difference between how you feel about the situations and how you would respond?
4. If there are inconsistencies between how you feel and how you think you would act, what steps can you take to move closer to how you want to feel?

Key Points for Facilitators to Elicit

1. Sometimes a person may find himself/herself facing an unexpected situation. Be honest and discrete in expressing feelings and confronting the situation.
2. Be aware of feelings and actions and try to make the two more compatible.

Handout 6.3
SCENARIOS

Directions for Participants

1. Read Scenario #1.
2. Discuss the scenario with the group in response to the facilitator's questions.
3. Repeat directions 1 and 2 for Scenarios #2 and #3.

Scenario #1

There is a teenager in your class of whom you are fond. One day the student approaches you and confides that he is gay and does not want anyone else to know. He is thinking of applying to the military and is asking for your support. How would you feel about this teenager confiding in you? What advice would you give him about the disclosure that he is gay? Should he tell his friends, his family? Would you counsel him regarding gay issues and the military? Would your opinion of him change?

Scenario #2

What is the attitude at your workplace toward homosexual employees? Would you say your work environment is very hostile, somewhat hostile, somewhat accepting, or very accepting toward homosexuals? How would you advise a colleague who "came out" to you? Would you recommend that your gay colleague "come out" to a supervisor, to fellow employees, to everyone? Should the employee bring his domestic partner to social functions? What other advice would you give your colleague?

Scenario #3

You unexpectedly run into a colleague and his partner holding hands. Both you and your colleague are caught off guard and hastily retreat from the situation. How do you respond to your colleague the next time you see him? Do you share this information with other colleagues? Has your opinion of your colleague changed?

Handout 6.3. Permission is granted to photocopy for classroom use.

Activity 6.4
PROBLEMS AND SOLUTIONS ASSOCIATED WITH GAYS AND LESBIANS IN EDUCATIONAL AND WORKPLACE SETTINGS

Objective: To identify specific problems and their solutions associated with gays and lesbians in educational and workplace settings
Estimated Time: 40 to 45 minutes
Materials Needed: Paper and pencils for participants

Directions for Facilitators

1. Organize participants into groups of five or six.
2. Instruct each group to compile a list of five problems relative to gays and lesbians in an educational or workplace setting. Provide the following examples:

   Example: "Considering the Federal Equal Access Act of 1984, what can be done about groups that protest the formation of a gay/lesbian club on a high school campus?"
   Example: "How can a corporation be sure that the people in charge of hiring are not discriminating against gay and lesbian applicants?"

   (Allow approximately 15 minutes for this part of the activity.)

3. After all groups have completed their lists, ask each group to exchange its list with another group. Then ask all groups to discuss their new lists and devise a solution to each of the problems. (Allow approximately 10 to 15 minutes for this part of the activity.)
4. When participants have finished this part of the activity, ask for a volunteer from each group to read two or three of the group's problems and solutions.
5. Facilitate discussion using the questions provided.

Questions for Discussion

1. How significant do you feel some of these problems are? Rank them in order of significance.

2. How easy would it be to implement the proposed solutions?
3. Has this exercise made you more sensitive to problems in the educational and workplace arenas? If yes, how?

Key Points for Facilitators to Elicit

1. Some problem areas may be very subtle and not as easily identified, such as the "glass ceiling."
2. Confronting some problem areas may be controversial and may engender conflict.

Activity 6.5
PROMOTING POSITIVE ATTITUDES AT SCHOOL
AND IN THE WORKPLACE

Objective: To identify activities and programs that can be implemented to pro-
mote positive attitude changes in schools and in the workplace
Estimated Time: 80 to 90 minutes
Materials Needed: Chart paper, markers, and masking tape; Handout 6.5 (Part
A): Promoting Positive Attitudes in the Workplace and/or Handout 6.5 (Part B):
Promoting Positive Attitudes in School

Directions for Facilitators

1. Organize participants into groups of six.
2. Distribute one copy of Handout 6.5 (Part A) or Handout 6.5 (Part B) to
   each group. (If the workshop is for corporate executives, use only Part A;
   if it is for school personnel, distribute Part A to half the groups and Part
   B to the remaining groups.)
3. Ask each group to follow the directions on the handout. (Allow
   45 minutes to complete this task.)
4. After the activity has been completed, ask each leader to post his or her
   group's findings.
5. Facilitate discussion. Below are some ideas to share with the large group
   if this information is not presented from the smaller groups. According to
   McNaught (1993), a systematic plan for eliminating discrimination
   against homosexual employees should include:

   1. an employment policy prohibiting discrimination based on sexual
      orientation,
   2. a safe work environment,
   3. education in the workplace about gay issues and AIDS,
   4. a benefits program for domestic partners,
   5. support of a homosexual support group,
   6. freedom for employees to fully participate in all aspects of corporate
      life, and
   7. public support of gay issues.

McNaught, B. (1993). *Gay issues in the workplace*. New York: St. Martin's Press.

Handout 6.5 (Part A)
PROMOTING POSITIVE ATTITUDES
IN THE WORKPLACE

Directions for Participants

1. Select a leader within your group.
2. For each of the following six categories, develop program content, ideas, or policies that you feel will help accentuate positive attitudes in the workplace. Be as specific and creative as possible in your brainstorming.
3. Once your group has completed the activity (approximately 45 minutes), have your group leader post your group's findings.
4. Prepare to discuss your group's ideas with the other workshop participants.

1. Identify topic ideas for an inservice workshop for employees, management, and family members/ domestic partners.

2. What counseling/Employee Assistance Program services should be offered in the workplace?

3. What services should be offered to domestic partners and what should company policy be regarding health coverage, life insurance, and disability?

4. What company policies should be in place for: maternity leave for homosexuals, single gay parents, leave for illness/death of domestic partners or their family members?

5. What policies should be implemented regarding homophobic behavior at work?

6. What can companies do to elicit greater acceptance of diversity and participation in corporate life?

Handout 6.5 (Part B)
PROMOTING POSITIVE ATTITUDES IN SCHOOL

Directions for Participants

1. Select a leader within your group.
2. For each of the following six categories, develop program content, ideas, or policies that you feel will help accentuate positive attitudes in the workplace. Be as specific and creative as possible in your brainstorming.
3. Once your group has completed the activity (approximately 45 minutes), have your group leader post your group's findings.
4. Prepare to discuss your group's ideas with the other workshop participants.

1. Identify topic ideas for an inservice workshop for faculty, students, and families.

2. What counseling services and resource materials should be offered to students in schools?

3. Identify ways in which gay issues in the workplace could be incorporated into a career day program.

4. Identify topics for student assemblies to sensitize students.

5. What types of self-help groups should be offered on your campus?

6. Make a list of speakers who would be appropriate for your student body.

CLOSETED GAYS AND LESBIANS

No matter when a person realizes and accepts the fact that his or her sexual orientation is different from the heterosexual majority, many decisions must be made. Society has taught, in obvious and subtle ways, that homosexuality and bisexuality are generally unacceptable. The first line of defense for many gays, lesbians, and bisexuals is to keep the realization private, but at certain points in their lives they must decide whom to tell and whom not to tell. Some of the deciding factors may involve acceptance by certain groups or individuals, securing and maintaining employment, or, literally, self-preservation. The decision to reveal one's sexual orientation or to remain closeted has both advantages and disadvantages.

Activity 7.1: Speculations Regarding the Lives of Closeted Gays and Lesbians gives participants a chance to think and talk about what it must be like for closeted gays and lesbians as they live, work, play, attend school, etc., in a hostile society. Activity 7.2: Interview: Senior Citizens in Retrospect consists of an interview of a gay senior citizen who describes what life has been like for him and his domestic partner as they lived closeted lives in our society. Activity 7.3: Special Problems of the Gay and Lesbian Elderly presents some real issues that face gays and lesbians and their partners when they are forced to deal with illness, death, and property distribution. This activity stimulates participants' thoughts and dialogue about the complicated legal protection of the rights of a gay or lesbian partner and the importance of protective workplace policies for gay and lesbian domestic partners. Activity 7.4: Case Study: Karen illustrates the emotional turmoil that can be caused by being closeted in the workplace.

Activity 7.1
SPECULATIONS REGARDING THE LIVES
OF CLOSETED GAYS AND LESBIANS

Objective: To give participants an opportunity to speculate on the daily lives of closeted gays and lesbians in various societal roles and to realize the special problems that exist for gays and lesbians living in a predominantly heterosexist society
Estimated Time: 45 to 50 minutes
Materials Needed: Handout 7.1: Speculations Regarding the Lives of Closeted Gays and Lesbians (one copy for each participant); chart paper, masking tape, and markers

Directions for Facilitators

1. Organize participants into groups of six.
2. Distribute Handout 7.1 to all participants.
3. Assign each group one of the categories from the handout and ask them to follow the directions listed. (Allow 15 minutes for this part of the activity.)
4. Ask the group leaders to post the charts and present the lists of descriptors to the entire group of participants.
5. Facilitate discussion.

Questions for Discussion

1. How do you think closeted gays and lesbians feel leading a dual lifestyle?
2. What impact does this have on their self-esteem? Personal achievements? Goals? Happiness?
3. What, if anything, have you learned about these issues from gay or lesbian friends, colleagues, students, or family members?

Key Points for Facilitators to Elicit

1. Living a closeted existence takes a toll on most aspects of a person's life.
2. People may not always be who they seem to be on the outside.

Handout 7.1
SPECULATIONS REGARDING THE LIVES
OF CLOSETED GAYS AND LESBIANS

Directions for Participants

1. Select a leader for your group.
2. After the facilitator has assigned a person from the list below, discuss what you think it would be like to be that closeted homosexual. Think in terms of (a) family life, (b) social life, (c) vocational or school life, and (d) peer expectations. (Discuss and chart as many descriptors as possible within 15 minutes.)
3. Post your chart and present your list of descriptors to the entire group of workshop participants.
4. Participate in the large-group discussion about each of the categories listed.

1. gay middle school student
2. lesbian high school student
3. gay college student
4. lesbian vice president of a major corporation
5. gay professional football player
6. gay member of the clergy
7. gay Olympic star
8. 25-year-old lesbian who is climbing the corporate ladder
9. lesbian executive secretary
10. lesbian police officer

Handout 7.1. Permission is granted to photocopy for classroom use.

Activity 7.2
INTERVIEW: SENIOR CITIZENS IN RETROSPECT

Objectives: To provide participants with a case history of a gay senior citizen who remained closeted all of his life; to sensitize participants to a closeted gay person's experience

Estimated Time: 30 to 35 minutes

Materials Needed: Two copies of Handout 7.2 (Part A): Interview; Handout 7.2 (Part B): Gay and Lesbian Senior Citizens in Retrospect (one copy for each participant)

Directions for Facilitators

1. Ask for two participant volunteers.
2. Present each volunteer with a copy of Handout 7.2 (Part A) and assign roles.
3. Ask the volunteers to be seated where all participants can easily see and hear them as they role-play the interview.
4. Introduce the volunteer participants and set the scene as follows: "What you will be hearing is the dialogue between an interviewer and David, a gay retired corporate executive who remained closeted throughout his schooling and professional career. He has lived with his gay domestic partner since they were both graduate students in Massachusetts in 1953."
5. Ask the volunteers to begin the dialogue.
6. After the interview is completed, distribute Handout 7.2 (Part B) to all participants and ask them to follow the directions given.
7. Allow participants enough time to reflect and write their answers, then lead a general discussion of the questions.

Questions for Discussion

1. Did David get what he deserved? Was being gay his choice?
2. What could David have done throughout his life to facilitate the acceptance of his sexual orientation by his parents, employers, and colleagues?
3. What advice would you have given David for handling his life?

Handout 7.2 (Part A)
INTERVIEW

Directions for Participants

1. Role-play the part of the interviewer or David, as assigned by the facilitator.
2. Read aloud the following script for all participants.

I = Interviewer, D = David

I: David, before we begin, I would like to thank you for granting this interview, which we hope will serve to give the audience some insight into the lives of closeted gays and lesbians who live and work in mainstream heterosexual environments. How old were you when you realized you were gay?

D: Well, to be perfectly honest, I felt "different" while I was in elementary school, but it wasn't until I was in seventh or eighth grade that I realized HOW different I was from the other boys. They were beginning to be interested in girls and I wasn't the least bit interested. I don't think anyone really noticed. I was preoccupied with playing sports and playing clarinet in the band and I was pretty active in a church youth group.

I: You were in high school in the late 1940s. . . . How did you handle the peer pressure to date girls?

D: In those days I could get away with just dating for school dances and some of the other major school activities, like basketball games. When I was a junior I was seriously attracted to boys, but I kept it to myself. There wasn't much information available about being gay. No one ever talked about it. I just knew I'd better protect my secret by dating. I never dated the same girl more than once or twice, because I was trying to avoid a "steady" relationship.

I: Was college any different?

D: It was much more complicated. I was on a fairly large campus and I thought living in a dormitory would give me some anonymity, but there was a lot of pressure from some of my friends in the dorm. They were always fixing me up with dates, so I went, but I never felt comfortable. I was really miserable in college and stayed by myself as much as possible.

I: You met your domestic partner in graduate school. Did you live together at that time?

D: Yes, we rented an apartment together. It wasn't unusual for two men to share an apartment while in school.

I: Were your parents curious about why you didn't have a special female relationship?

D: No. They were just anxious for me to finish my education and get settled in a job. By the time I was in grad school, I felt estranged from my parents. They really didn't know me and there was very little communication. We were just polite to one another. I guess I was concerned that they might start asking personal questions and I was trying to avoid a confrontation by staying away from them.

I: What was your domestic partner's name?

D: Russ.

I: What happened after graduate school?

D: Both of us found positions in upstate New York. Russ was an architecture major and I had my MBA. I was hired by a large firm with offices around the world and it's the only firm I've worked for. By the time I was 37, I was a senior executive officer. Eventually, Russ became a partner in his firm.

I: Were you closeted all that time?

D: Yes, both of us were.

I: How did you manage to pull that off?

D: It was very difficult, but necessary.

I: What do you mean by difficult?

D: Well, both of our immediate superiors were very homophobic and we knew we would never move up the corporate ladder if they knew the truth. We used up a lot of energy trying to separate our private lives from our corporate lives. The first thing we did was move about 25 miles outside of the city. We bought an old farmhouse and renovated it. We had our own friends and only socialized with our business associates when it was absolutely necessary. We had several lesbian friends who attended company social events with us and we reciprocated. One of the women was a college administrator and needed a male escort for all sorts of college functions.

I: How did you feel about "living the lie"?

D: I hated every moment of it. You have no idea how complicated your life can get. There is a lot of anxiety connected with hiding who you really are and living two different lives. One time Russ drove to New York City on business and was involved in a bad accident with a drunk driver. Russ was unconscious. They rushed him to the nearest hospital. They found one of his business cards in his wallet and contacted his boss who called Russ' parents in Trenton, New Jersey. Meanwhile, I hadn't heard from Russ, who always called when he reached his destination, and I was frantic. It was two days before I knew what happened.

I: Why didn't his parents call you?

D: They did, but they waited 48 hours. Several months prior to the accident they had confronted

Russ about being gay and when he admitted it, his father became violent and threw him out of the house. They hated me and said it was my fault he was gay. They threatened to call the president of my firm. Fortunately, they never did it. Anyway, this is why they didn't contact me right away. I don't think they ever realized what a cruel decision they made. There was never a reconciliation between Russ and his parents. It's hard to believe, isn't it, that parents could be so homophobic that they would turn against their own son?

I: How did your living situation restrict the freedom of you and Russ all those years?

D: Pretending there isn't a significant person in your life presents all kinds of social and emotional problems.

I: Such as?

D: Well, just like any two people sharing a life together, there were frequent crises. All those years there were periods of illness requiring Russ or me to take responsibility for care and it was always hard to leave the office or not to report for work. It always meant lying about the actual situation. When our colleagues had health crises at home, they simply announced it and had the sympathy and support of their superiors. The thing is, both of us have lived through a lot of emotional crises, such as the deaths of our parents, and we couldn't even discuss it with anyone in our offices without having them get involved with our private lives. You just get very paranoid about being discovered. During these emotional upheavals it was almost impossible to even have private telephone conversations with one another. We always had to guard against the curiosity of our fellow workers.

I: You must have had to entertain the people in your firm. What did you do about this?

D: It's true, we did have to entertain them. It just meant one of us had to leave the house. We only entertained when it was absolutely necessary; it was too complicated.

I: Now that you're both retired, how are your lives different?

D: We have sold the house in the country and moved back to the city where most of our friends live. Life is much, much easier. We are living openly now that we don't have to worry about job security. An enormous burden has been lifted from our shoulders. In addition to our gay and lesbian friends, we have cultivated a number of straight friends who are accepting of our relationship. In a way it has been a difficult adjustment for both of us, after being closeted for so many years. The habit of hiding is haunting.

I: How do you perceive the changes in the present younger generation of gays and lesbians?

D: In some respects life is a little easier for them. At least there is some dialogue in our society concerning gays and lesbians. There are a lot of political activists who are trying to promote tolerance and acceptance. The population at large has become more knowledgeable, there are more mainstream gays and lesbians coming out and serving as positive role models for the younger generation of gays and lesbians, and there is some education going on in secondary schools and colleges. Just like any other minority group, we have to continue to fight for our human rights.

I: Have things changed in the workplace? Is it any easier for gay and lesbian employees to live out in the open?

D: Well, it all depends on where they live and the attitudes of their employers. There are a number of "gay-friendly" corporations that make the fact known to potential employees and, of course, many qualified gays and lesbians are hired by these companies, knowing they may live openly without discrimination. In many cases, their domestic partners are covered by benefits and company antidiscrimination policies are in place. But my guess is that most employers will not knowingly hire a gay or lesbian, regardless of qualifications. This attitude results in closeted gay and lesbian employees who are forced to live a lie socially and in the workplace. General tolerance and acceptance is still a long way off.

I: How would you predict the future of today's gay and lesbian youth?

D: It's hard to predict what it will be like in future decades. Right now there is a strong movement that resists human rights for the gay and lesbian minority, because it is driven by the philosophy that being gay or lesbian is a matter of choice. If scientific inquiry proves this philosophy is incorrect, it MAY make a substantial difference in some attitudes.

I: I have just one more question: How do you think your sexual orientation affected your achievement in the educational setting and/or your professional work?

D: School was always a haven for me. I always loved learning and excelled all the way through school. It was something I did well and no one could take it away from me. I think it was a way of storing recognition and acceptance . . . sort of a bank account. I felt I would always need to balance the social ostracism. So far as the workplace is concerned, even though I have had a successful career, I think my sexual orientation prevented me from taking professional risks, so I remained with the same firm where I felt somewhat safe; the unknown was too threatening.

I: David, our time is just about up. Thanks so much for your honesty in answering my questions. Let's hope this interview has helped the audience understand some of the decisions that have to be made by gays and lesbians who live and work in a homophobic environment.

Handout 7.2 (Part B)
GAY AND LESBIAN SENIOR CITIZENS IN RETROSPECT

Directions for Participants

1. Jot down some notes that will enable you to participate in a general discussion of the following questions and statement.
2. Share your notes with the entire group during the discussion.

1. What questions do you have relative to the interview?

_____

_____

_____

2. Compare and contrast your feelings from before and after the interview.

_____

_____

_____

3. What have you learned from the interview?

_____

_____

_____

4. How have any of your perceptions changed?

_____

_____

_____

Activity 7.3
SPECIAL PROBLEMS OF THE GAY
AND LESBIAN ELDERLY

Objective: To create an awareness of the special problems of gay and lesbian senior citizens

Estimated Time: 20 to 30 minutes

Materials Needed: Handout 7.3: Special Problems of the Gay and Lesbian Elderly

Directions for Facilitators

1. Using Handout 7.3, present some issues that develop from living closeted lives.
2. Facilitate discussion using the questions provided.

Questions for Discussion

1. Should young gays and lesbians be aware of these special problems of the gay and lesbian elderly?
2. If you believe an awareness is important for gay and lesbian youth, how could they be made aware in educational settings?
3. How are these special problems of the gay and lesbian elderly related to the workplace?
4. How do you feel about the facts that have been presented?
5. What steps might you take to effect change?

Handout 7.3
SPECIAL PROBLEMS OF THE GAY
AND LESBIAN ELDERLY

Directions for Participants

1. Review the following list of problems that have been associated with gay and lesbian elderly.
2. Be prepared to discuss each problem with the rest of the workshop participants.

1. Many older gays and lesbians have been prematurely placed in nursing and personal care homes because their children or families would not accept their sexual orientation and would not help care for them as their health failed.

2. In right-to-die and competency issues, a domestic partner is treated as no more than a close friend.

3. If a gay or lesbian should die without a will, the state generally awards the person's estate to his or her family, not to the partner, despite wishes to the contrary.

4. Juries often side with families contesting wills over partners of the same sex.

5. Some courts have ruled that companies can refuse to pay benefits to surviving partners of gay and lesbian employees, even if the company has a policy that bans discrimination on the basis of sexual orientation.

6. Gay and lesbian lifetime partners have been denied hospital visitation rights by families who did not accept the sexual orientation of the hospitalized family member.

7. Lifetime gay and lesbian partners have been denied participation in the burial decisions concerning their partners.

Activity 7.4
CASE STUDY: KAREN

Objective: To help participants understand the emotional turmoil experienced by closeted gays and lesbians who are terrified of being "discovered"
Estimated Time: 40 to 50 minutes
Materials Needed: Handout 7.4: Case Study: Karen (one copy for each group)

Directions for Facilitators

1. Organize participants into groups of four.
2. Distribute Handout 7.4 (one copy to each group).
3. Ask participants to follow the directions on the handout and complete the activity within 20 to 25 minutes.
4. After the allotted time, ask each group to join one other group and compare and discuss their answers to the case study questions. (Allow 10 to 15 minutes for this part of the activity.)
5. Ask participants to return to their seats.
6. Facilitate group discussion using the questions provided.

Questions for Discussion

1. What are the advantages to being closeted? What are the disadvantages?
2. What suggestions do you have for legislation that would protect gays and lesbians in workplace or educational settings?
3. What role could labor or professional organizations play in encouraging closeted gay and lesbian employees to "come out" on the job?

Key Points for Facilitators to Elicit

1. In a homophobic environment, most gays and lesbians decide to hide their sexual orientation and adapt in any way possible to protect themselves and their livelihoods.
2. It may be to the advantage of employers to allow gay and lesbian employees to be honest about their sexual orientations.
3. Most heterosexuals have difficulty understanding the intimidation gays and lesbians feel and why so many make the decision to remain closeted.

Handout 7.4
CASE STUDY: KAREN

Directions for Participants

1. Select a group leader.
2. The group leader will read the case study aloud to the group and facilitate discussion and answering of the case study questions. (You will have 20 to 25 minutes to complete this activity.)
3. When time is called, you will be asked to join another group to compare and discuss the case study questions.

Karen, a closeted lesbian, grew up in a midwestern urban area where she attended private schools and eventually earned a Ph.D. in chemistry from a prestigious university. While in graduate school, she and another woman established a committed relationship and decided, after graduate school, to seek employment and residency in the same geographic location.

Karen was hired by a pharmaceutical corporation in a major city to direct an important project. Shortly thereafter her domestic partner found employment in the same city and together they leased an apartment. Karen quickly realized she was working in a homophobic environment, but she decided she would not jeopardize her career by challenging the derogatory remarks and jokes that circulated in the workplace.

One of the vice-presidents was assigned to oversee her project and they spent a lot of time together in meetings and business luncheons. He became enamored with Karen and pursued her for several months. He asked her for social dates several times, which she politely refused, giving him various excuses. At one time, he casually asked if she lived alone. Fearful that he was becoming suspicious, and caught off guard, Karen answered in the affirmative. He had flowers delivered to her office on her birthday and continued to ask for dates, which she refused. Angered by the rejections, he found her home address in her personnel file, visited the building, and saw her name along with the name of her domestic partner on the mailbox.

He called her to his office the next day and made sexual advances, which she rejected. He confronted her with the "mailbox information" and asked if she were a lesbian. Frightened and angered by his accusation, she ran from his office and went home. The next day she announced to the president that she was leaving the company and would be looking for another position. He said he already knew the reason and, although she was an exemplary project director, he would never have hired her if he had known the truth about her sexual orientation. He also warned her that he would be truthful if he received any requests for job references for her.

1. How could this situation affect the rest of Karen's career? _____

_____

_____

2. What could Karen have done differently to maintain her self-respect and dignity and to protect her professional career? _____

_____

_____

3. What advice would you give Karen relative to the pursuit of her next job? _____

_____

_____

Handout 7.4. Permission is granted to photocopy for classroom use.

PREPARING GAY AND LESBIAN STUDENTS FOR THE WORKPLACE

Gay and lesbian students in our secondary schools and colleges know they are living in a predominantly homophobic society. Consequently, most decide to remain "invisible" and keep silent regarding their sexual orientation. Educational systems have responded positively to the unique needs of many different minority groups through policy and curricula changes; however, the invisibility of most gay and lesbian students makes it difficult for educational decision-makers to realize that the needs of 10% of their students are being neglected. In addition, many people involved with schools fail to recognize the elusive connections between the neglect of the needs of these students and many of the problems that plague school systems, such as academic failure, absenteeism, dropouts, alcohol/drug abuse, violence, and teenage pregnancy.

One of the goals of American secondary schools is to contribute to the preparation of students for the workplace. The multidimensional nature of this goal makes it necessary to address the unique needs of minority groups, one of which is students who are homosexual or bisexual. Activity 8.1: Nurturing Self-Esteem and Communicating the Existence of a Safe Environment emphasizes the importance of self-esteem enhancement for gay and lesbian students and the need for educators to communicate the idea that the school environment is safe for gays and lesbians. Activity 8.2: Workshop to Prepare Gay and Lesbian Students for the Workplace calls on participants to role-play a board of directors that will design a workplace policy for gay and lesbian employees. Activity 8.3: Gay-Friendly Companies creates an awareness of a trend in the corporate world to become "gay friendly" and includes a sample list of American gay-friendly companies.

Activity 8.1
NURTURING SELF-ESTEEM AND COMMUNICATING
THE EXISTENCE OF A SAFE ENVIRONMENT

Objective: To help participants understand the importance of enhancing the self-esteem of gay and lesbian students and communicating the existence of a safe environment
Estimated Time: 55 to 60 minutes
Materials Needed: Handout 8.1: Nurturing Self-Esteem and Communicating the Existence of a Safe Environment (one copy for each group)

Directions for Facilitators

1. Organize participants into groups of five.
2. Present the Background Information to participants. (Try not to allow discussion at this time.)
3. Distribute Handout 8.1 (one copy to each group) and ask participants to follow the directions on the handout. (Allow 20 minutes for this activity.)
4. After the allotted time, ask each group to identify a few of their suggestions.
5. After all groups have participated, read the following information and invite participants' discussion as the list is presented.
    *   Disciplines students who use derogatory terms such as "fag," "queer," and "lezzie." Gently explains to the class why they are not appropriate.
    *   Uses language that indicates an awareness of sexual diversity.
    *   Where appropriate in the curriculum, discusses the concept of "diversity" and its advantages in a democratic society (e.g., multiculturalism, individual talents, career choices . . .).
    *   Appropriate to the subject matter being taught, discusses the contribution of gays and lesbians (e.g., Leonardo da Vinci, Sophocles, Socrates, Aristotle, Lewis Carroll, A. E. Houseman, Tchaikovsky, Tennessee Williams, Somerset Maugham, Greg Louganis, Cole Porter, Elton John, and others).
    *   Where appropriate, discusses the origins and effects of prejudice and bigotry.
    *   Speaks out against harassment.
    *   Indicates that "humor" at the expense of gays and lesbians is offensive.
    *   Where appropriate, discusses the concept of "stereotyping."
    *   Actively listens to students.

- Conveys commitment to confidentiality in student–teacher conferences.
- Conveys respect for all students at all times.
- Insists students respect one another.
- Provides experiences that will allow all students to feel successful.
- Reinforces positive classroom behavior.
- Emphasizes success and deemphasizes failure.
- Knows students as individuals.
- Uses cooperative learning strategies.

6. Facilitate discussion using the questions provided.

Questions for Discussion

1. Why is it crucial for educators to realize that the majority of gays and lesbians do not fit the stereotypes?
2. What are some student behaviors that may indicate improved self-esteem?
3. How can school boards and administrators be convinced of the urgency for action to help gay and lesbian students?
4. How is the nurturing of students' self-esteem connected to their preparation for the workplace?

Key Points for Facilitators to Elicit

1. Low self-esteem is characteristic of many gay and lesbian students. A contributing factor is the shame and guilt imposed by living in a homophobic society. Frequently, gay and lesbian students respond to their feelings by acting out in negative ways and using various defense and escape mechanisms.
2. Educators are in a position to help students with low self-esteem through efforts to change how students think and feel about themselves.
3. Changes in the educational policies of school systems can help prevent low self-esteem among gay and lesbian students. Two significant policy initiatives involve breaking the pervasive silence in schools relative to sexual minorities and providing a safe environment for gay and lesbian students.
4. Guided by the public educational goal to prepare students for the workplace in a democratic society, schools are obliged to provide opportunities for all students to develop their potential and talents, enabling them to creatively and productively participate in the working world.

BACKGROUND INFORMATION

The research literature on gay and lesbian youth reports that low self-esteem is endemic within the gay and lesbian adolescent population and that this promotes risky behaviors such as academic apathy and failure, depression, suicide, running away from home, alcohol/drug abuse, and sexual encounters that may lead to diseases. It would be difficult to find an American school that did not have as one of its documented primary goals "to enhance the self-esteem of all students." Professional educators are aware that learning is a function of self-esteem, as are life and health and humanness itself.

Training for educators emphasizes the importance of providing daily opportunities for enhancing the self-esteem of students as they participate in curricular and extracurricular activities. As a legitimate part of the educating process, school personnel make the effort to help students feel liked, wanted, accepted, capable, dignified, and worthy. Gay and lesbian students hear the message almost everywhere that they are outcasts of society. There are keenly aware of society's intolerance for differences and the strong homophobia among their peers, and school is a place where "fag" and "queer" are constantly heard in the hallways, along with threats of violence against anyone thought to be gay or lesbian.

This hostility frightens gay and lesbian adolescents and leaves them uncertain about their own worth. Their self-esteem plummets and they realize they must hide their sexual orientation from everyone, including their families. Fearful of being labeled "different" and afraid they will be rejected if their sexual orientation is discovered, they pretend to be someone they are not. These circumstances force them to deal with their emotional turmoil in isolation.

Although these students are not often identifiable, if educators simply assume their presence and take the necessary steps to allay their fears and convey an attitude of trust and caring, these students may take the risk of reaching out for help.

Background Information for Activity 8.1.   Permission is granted to photocopy for classroom use.

Handout 8.1
NURTURING SELF-ESTEEM AND COMMUNICATING
THE EXISTENCE OF A SAFE ENVIRONMENT

Directions for Participants

1. Within your group, collaborate and discuss the question below.
2. Write as many specific suggestions as possible. (You will have 20 minutes to complete this activity.)

Given the "invisibility" of most gays and lesbians in classrooms, what could sensitive and aware teachers say or do in their classrooms to nurture self-esteem and to let these anonymous students know it is safe to approach the teacher for counsel?

1. _____
2. _____
3. _____
4. _____
5. _____
6. _____
7. _____
8. _____
9. _____
10. _____
11. _____

Handout 8.1. Permission is granted to photocopy for classroom use.

Activity 8.2
WORKSHOP TO PREPARE GAY AND LESBIAN
STUDENTS FOR THE WORKPLACE

Objective: To develop a "recipe" for a workshop that could be initiated in the participants' educational setting or workplace
Estimated Time: 90 to 95 minutes
Materials Needed: Chart paper, markers, and masking tape; Handout 8.2: Designing a Workplace Policy (one copy for each participant)

Directions for Facilitators

1. Identify five participants to become the Board of Directors of a major corporation who have been invited to a local college to talk with prospective employees about the following topic: "How can you best prepare for corporate employment if you are gay or lesbian?"
2. Distribute Handout 8.2 to all participants.
3. Instruct the Board of Directors to develop a workshop for this three-hour discussion. (This should take approximately 60 minutes.) Assign the rest of the participants the task of observing the process, taking notes for additional suggestions for inclusion in the workshop, and commenting on the group process and attitudes that were conveyed during the discussion.
4. Have the Board of Directors write its ideas on chart paper and post for everyone to see. This should be in the form of a workshop outline that can be presented to the larger group.
5. Open the discussion to the group using the questions provided. Modify the workshop outline, if necessary, based on the suggestions and comments.
6. Provide each participant with a copy of the final workshop outline that was generated.

Questions for Discussion

1. How did you feel about the process you observed as the Board of Directors developed the workshop? What do you think were the barriers to the process and what steps could have been taken to overcome them?
2. Were there topics that should have been covered in the workshop that the Board of Directors omitted?

3. What suggestions would you have for modifying this workshop?
4. What obstacles do you feel this Board of Directors would encounter if it presented this workshop?
5. What modifications can be made in this workshop to tailor it for presentation in your specific work environment?

Handout 8.2
DESIGNING A WORKPLACE POLICY

Directions for Participants

1. Read the list of topics below for possible inclusion in the workshop.
2. Be prepared to take part in the large-group discussion upon completion of the activity.

1. Should the employee/student come out or not? Partially out with select employees such as the boss?
2. If the employee/student chooses to come out, how should it be done?
3. What about benefits for domestic partners? Should this question be asked? If so, when? And how do you obtain this information if you do not ask?
4. What about leave benefits for such things as maternity or crisis (e.g., illness, funeral)?
5. What are the behavioral expectations of the company? Can I be out as a representative of the corporation or does that pose a conflict for the company?
6. What are the policies for sensitizing straight employees to workplace policies—i.e., workplace sensitivity?
7. What is the policy regarding social events? Can I bring my partner or date?
8. Will sexual orientation make a difference regarding promotion?
9. Should employees be permitted to participate in public gay and lesbian events such as Gay Pride?
10. How does the company deal with homophobia at work? Are there workplace policies?
11. What legal protections are in place (e.g., antidiscrimination policies and laws protecting workers)?

12. What signals might indicate acceptance/nonacceptance?
13. How do I identify "gay-friendly" corporations?
14. What questions should I ask/not ask during the interview process?

Handout 8.2. Permission is granted to photocopy for classroom use.

Activity 8.3
GAY-FRIENDLY COMPANIES

Objective: To create an awareness of a trend in the corporate world to become "gay friendly"
Estimated Time: 45 to 50 minutes
Materials Needed: Handout 8.3: A Sample List of Gay-Friendly Companies (one copy for each participant)

Directions for Facilitators

1. Organize participants into groups of four or six. Instruct participants to work in pairs.
2. Select information from the Background Information and share it with participants.
3. Distribute Handout 8.3 (one copy to each participant) and ask participants to follow the directions on the handout. (Allow 30 minutes for completion of the activity.)
4. After the allotted time, review and discuss participants' answers by soliciting volunteers.
   (*Note*: If participants have had difficulty determining generalizations for Question #1 of Handout 8.3, four are listed below.)

   a. Most of the companies listed have employees numbering in the thousands, tens of thousands, and hundreds of thousands, which means some major corporations are responding to the needs of their gay and lesbian employees. (Ask participants to speculate concerning the reasons.)
   b. Most of the companies listed are in the northeast and on the west coast of the United States. (Ask participants to speculate concerning the reasons.)
   c. Seven prestigious universities are listed. (Ask participants to speculate concerning the reasons.)
   d. Almost half of the companies listed (14) are high-tech companies. (Ask participants to speculate concerning the reasons.)

Key Points for Facilitators to Elicit

1. Discrimination against gays and lesbians is widespread in today's American workplace and manifests itself in obvious and subtle ways.

2. Misconceptions and homophobic attitudes cause many employers to exclude qualified and talented gays and lesbians from the workplace, based solely on sexual orientation.
3. Individual gay and lesbian employees who were closeted when hired and who proved valuable to their employers have courageously "come out" in their workplaces to negotiate for domestic-partner benefits, nondiscriminatory policies, diversity training, and the establishment of gay and lesbian employee groups.
4. There is a slow-growing number of gay-friendly American companies attracting qualified and talented gays and lesbians as potential employees.
5. Dissemination of information to secondary schools and colleges about gay-friendly employers can be a strong motivating force in preparing gay and lesbian students for the workplace.

BACKGROUND INFORMATION

Ed Mickens, author of *The 100 Best Companies for Gay Men and Lesbians* (1994, Pocket Books, New York), has identified 100 American companies that have earned the title of "gay friendly." Mickens used the following four criteria in evaluating and rating the companies:

1. A written nondiscrimination policy that was enforced.
2. If diversity training was offered, it included gay and lesbian issues.
3. A gay and lesbian employee group recognized by the employer.
4. The availability of benefits for domestic partners (e.g., medical, dental, bereavement, and sickness leave).

The employers included in this activity represent less than half those listed by Mickens and were chosen for their easy identification by most participants.

Background Information for Activity 8.3.   Permission is granted to photocopy for classroom use.

Handout 8.3
A SAMPLE LIST OF GAY-FRIENDLY COMPANIES

Directions for Participants

1. With your partner, study the list below and answer the questions that follow.
2. Compare your answers with those of two other partners in your group. (You will have approximately 30 minutes to complete this activity.)

Company	Location of Headquarters	Number of Employees
1. AT&T	Basking Ridge, NJ	300,000
2. Apple Computer Inc.	Cupertino, CA	14,500
3. Ben & Jerry's Inc.	Waterbury, VT	600
4. Blue Cross & Blue Shield of Massachusetts	Boston, MA	6,000
5. The Boston Globe	Boston, MA	3,400
6. Children's Hospital	Boston, MA	4,200
7. Columbia University	New York, NY	14,000
8. Digital Equipment Co.	Maynard, MA	113,000
9. Walt Disney Co.	Burbank, CA	50,000
10. E.I. duPont de Nemours	Wilmington, DE	125,000
11. Federal National Mortgage Association	Washington, DC	3,000
12. Genentech Inc.	San Francisco, CA	2,400

Company	Location of Headquarters	Number of Employees
13. Greenpeace Intl.	Washington, DC	1,000
14. Harvard University	Cambridge, MA	15,000
15. HBO/Time Warner Inc.	New York, NY	1,000
16. Eastman Kodak	Rochester, NY	132,000
17. Levi Strauss & Co.	San Francisco, CA	23,000
18. Lotus Development	Cambridge, MA	3,200
19. Massachusetts Institute of Technology	Cambridge, MA	8,000
20. Microsoft Corp.	Redmond, WA	12,000
21. National Organization for Women	Washington, DC	30
22. National Public Radio	Washington, DC	400
23. New York University	New York, NY	12,000
24. Oracle Corp.	Redwood Shores, CA	10,600
25. Public Broadcasting— PBS	Washington, DC	350
26. Charles Schwab & Co.	San Francisco, CA	4,000
27. Silicon Graphics	Mountain View, CA	3,800
28. Stanford University	Palo Alto, CA	9,000
29. Sun Microsystems	Mountain View, CA	13,000

Company	Location of Headquarters	Number of Employees
30. University of Chicago	Chicago, IL	6,400
31. University of Minnesota	St. Paul, MN	17,000
32. Viacom Intl. Inc.	New York, NY	5,000
33. WGBH	Boston, MA	900
34. WQED	Pittsburgh, PA	160

From Mickens, E. (1994). *The 100 Best Companies for Gay Men and Lesbians*. New York: Pocket Books.

Questions for Discussion

1. What generalizations can you make from studying list?
2. Would this kind of information be helpful at the high school level? If so, how?
3. How could this kind of information benefit undergraduate- and graduate-level college students?
4. Congress has outlawed discrimination on the basis of race, color, religion, gender, national origin, or disability. If a federal law added "sexual orientation," in what ways might the law affect the workplace and/or gay and lesbian employees?

Handout 8.3. Permission is granted to photocopy for classroom use.

STUDENTS WITH GAY OR LESBIAN PARENTS

This section is intended to increase participants' awareness of the growing number of children who have gay or lesbian parents and to explore how these "alternative families" influence change in our social institutions. Activity 9.1: Statistics Related to Gay and Lesbian Parents establishes a statistical framework and creates dialogue concerning possible changes required to address the needs of children with gay or lesbian parents. Activities 9.2: Gay and Lesbian Parental Issues, 9.3: Parents' Sexuality and Its Impact on Children, and 9.4: Educators Working with Gay and Lesbian Parents focus on the educational setting and the specific needs of students who have one or two homosexual parents. Workshop participants will have the opportunity to react to real situations that commonly occur in public, private, and parochial schools.

Activity 9.1
STATISTICS RELATED TO GAY
AND LESBIAN PARENTS

Objectives: To establish a statistical frame of reference regarding gay and lesbian parents in the United States; to explore how alternative families may influence change in the workplace, in education, and in jurisprudence
Estimated Time: 40 to 45 minutes
Materials Needed: Handout 9.1: Statistics: Gay and Lesbian Parents (one copy for each group); six prepared 3 × 5 index cards (see Directions for Facilitators)

Directions for Facilitators

1. Organize participants into six groups.
2. Distribute Handout 9.1 (one to each group) and review the statistics with participants. (Try to avoid discussion at this point.)
3. Pass out the prepared 3 × 5 cards, one to each group. Each card will bear one of the following questions:

> What implications do the statistics on Handout 9.1 have for 21st-century workplace politics?
> What implications do the statistics on Handout 9.1 have for 21st-century educational curricula?
> What implications do the statistics on Handout 9.1 have for 21st-century local, state, and federal law?
> What implications do the statistics on Handout 9.1 have for 21st-century training for teachers?
> What implications do the statistics on Handout 9.1 have for 21st-century school board policies?
> What implications do the statistics on Handout 9.1 have for 21st-century guidance counselors?

4. Ask participants to follow the directions given on the handout. (Allow approximately 20 minutes for this part of the activity.)
5. After the allotted time, ask a representative from each group to report the question assigned to his or her group and the three responses.
6. Facilitate discussion.

Questions for Discussion

1. Should anything special be done to address the needs of students of gay or lesbian parents?
2. Do you think children of gay or lesbian parents may have special needs?
3. What changes may need to occur to accommodate the needs of children of gay or lesbian parents?
4. What is the effect of the general population being unaware of the statistics regarding gay and lesbian parents?

Handout 9.1
STATISTICS: GAY AND LESBIAN PARENTS

Directions for Participants

1. Follow along as the facilitator reads the following statistics.
2. Read the question assigned to your group by the facilitator and discuss the question within your group.
3. Reach a consensus within your group regarding at least three different specific responses to the question. (You will have approximately 20 minutes to complete this activity.)
4. When called upon, have someone from your group report the assigned question and responses to the rest of the workshop participants.
5. Participate in the large-group discussion.

1. In 1992 it was estimated there were between one million and five million lesbian mothers in the United States (Patterson, 1992).

2. In 1992 it was estimated there were between one million and three million gay fathers in the United States (Patterson, 1992).

3. An estimated six million to fourteen million children in America have a lesbian or gay parent (Patterson, 1992).

4. An estimated 10,000 American children are being raised by lesbians who became pregnant through artificial insemination (Turque et al., 1992).

5. Thirty-five studies conducted between 1976 and 1991 indicated that children of gay and lesbian parents are no more likely to become homosexuals than are children of heterosexuals, and they are just as well adjusted (Gross, 1991).

References

Gross, J. (1991, February 11). New challenge of youth: Growing up in a gay home. *New York Times.*

Patterson, C. (1992). Children of lesbian and gay parents. *Child Development, 63.*

Turque, W., et al. (1992, September 14). Gays under fire. *Newsweek.*

Handout 9.1.   Permission is granted to photocopy for classroom use.

Activity 9.2
GAY AND LESBIAN PARENTAL ISSUES

Objective: To identify some of the issues for students who have one or more parents who are homosexual

Estimated Time: 30 to 35 minutes

Materials Needed: Chart paper, markers, and masking tape for participants; Handout 9.2: Gay and Lesbian Parental Issues (one copy for each group)

Directions for Facilitators

1.   Organize participants into five groups.
2.   Distribute Handout 9.2 to each group.
3.   Assign one of the questions from the handout to each group and ask them to follow the directions given on the handout.
4.   Facilitate discussion on each question.

Key Points for Facilitators to Elicit

1.   Students of gay or lesbian parents may send signals to educators regarding their gay or lesbian parent.
2.   Educators need to be sensitive to the issues faced by students who have a gay or lesbian parent.

Handout 9.2
GAY AND LESBIAN PARENTAL ISSUES

Directions for Participants

1. Answer the question (from below) assigned to your group.
2. Once consensus has been reached, select someone from your group to post your group's response to the question and report to the larger group.
3. Participate in the discussion of each question.

1. What problems can you anticipate for students with homosexual parents?

2. What signals might children with homosexual parents send to educators about how the alternative family is influencing them?

3. When one or both of a student's parents are homosexual, how may school behavior be affected (i.e., social and academic)?

4. When one or both of a student's parents are homosexual and school behavior is affected, what actions should teachers take? (i.e., Should teachers involve support personnel such as the guidance counselor, other teachers, or outside sources such as a psychologist, a clergyman, a physician, or others?)

5. When one or both of a student's parents are homosexual and school behavior is affected, should teachers contact the child's parents? Which parent: the primary residential parent, the homosexual parent, or the straight parent? Should the teacher confer with the student? Why or why not?

Handout 9.2. Permission is granted to photocopy for classroom use.

Activity 9.3
PARENTS' SEXUALITY AND ITS IMPACT
ON CHILDREN

Objective: To identify potential dialogue a teacher might have with a student, a counselor, or a parent in discussing the issue of a parent's sexuality and its impact on a student
Estimated Time: 45 to 50 minutes
Materials Needed: Paper and pencils for participants; Handout 9.3: Parental Scenarios (one copy for each participant)

Directions for Facilitators

1. Organize participants into groups of four.
2. Distribute Handout 9.3 to all participants and ask them to follow the directions given on the handout. (Allow approximately 35 minutes for this part of the activity.)
3. Facilitate large-group discussion.

Questions for Discussion

1. How do you feel about the scenarios you observed?
2. What could have been some alternative responses?
3. What guidelines might have helped the teacher?

Key Points for Facilitators to Elicit

1. Parents' sexuality affects their children.
2. Atypical classroom behavior needs to be explored more thoroughly.
3. Be relaxed and comfortable in your dialogues with others. If you cannot, seek assistance.

Handout 9.3
PARENTAL SCENARIOS

Directions for Participants

1. Identify within your group two people to be the active participants and two to act as observers for the first scenario.
2. The two active participants will role-play Scenario #1 while the other two group members observe and take notes.
3. The two observers should then provide feedback to the two who role-played on how they might have improved their role-play.
4. For Scenario #2, the active participants become the observers and the observers do the role-playing. Repeat steps 2 and 3 for each scenario, switching duties each time, until all scenarios have been role-played. (You will have approximately 35 minutes to complete this activity.)
5. Return to the large group and discuss what occurred and what you learned.

Scenario #1

You are a teacher. David, one of your students, is experiencing academic difficulties not only in your class but in other classes as well. Although David is bright and has done well in previous grades and classes, you observe that he has become withdrawn in class, he is not interacting with his peers in the hallways, and he has become extremely sensitive to comments from others. How would you reach out to David? Role-play your interaction with him. At some point during this dialogue David will reveal that he has just learned his mother is a lesbian. How will you respond to him? What will you do with this information?

Scenario #2

You are a teacher. One of your students, John, is engaging in flamboyant sexual behavior in class. He is very effeminate in his mannerisms and calls attention to himself by the way he dresses and the statements he makes. He is subject to ridicule and teasing by the other students. Although outwardly he does not appear to be bothered by this reaction from his peers, you are uncomfortable with this continued interaction among your students and want to do something to assist John. You call his father to discuss the issue and when John's father arrives for the meeting you realize that he is exhibiting the same behavior as his son. Role-play how you would handle this.

Scenario #3

Your student, Tom, has just come to you and asked if he can tell you something, but he demands a promise not to divulge this information to anyone. Tom says if you don't promise not to tell anyone, he will not talk with you. You agree to keep the information confidential. He then shares that he recently learned his mother is a lesbian. He is devastated by the news and does not have anyone in whom he can confide. If his father learns of his mother's lesbianism, Tom is afraid of his father's potential reaction, because his father is known to have violent tendencies. Tom is afraid if his friends learn about this, he will be ridiculed and no longer have any friends. Furthermore, he is afraid information like this would spread like "wild fire." He is afraid of telling his girlfriend for fear she will leave him. Consequently, Tom is thinking of running away from home or killing himself. What can you say to Tom and how can you discuss this with a counselor when you have been sworn to confidentiality? Role-play your discussion with Tom.

Scenario #4

Each student has been asked to invite his or her parents to an upcoming class event. Mary is a bit uncomfortable about having both parents invited to this event and asks if she can just invite her mother. You know she has a father and it is against school policy, in cases of divorce, not to inform both parents of school activities that involve a child. How do you handle this situation? Role-play your conversation with Mary.

The time for the school activity has arrived. Mary's mother has come alone and Mary's father has come with his boyfriend. You notice that Mary is very uncomfortable and is spending the majority of her time in the bathroom. She is not interacting with her friends and her mother is engaging in conversation with other parents and does not seem aware of Mary's feelings. Role-play how you would handle this interaction with Mary and with Mary's father and his friend.

Scenario #5

Judy's mother has come to the school to tell you she is moving in with a person of the same sex and wants you to know about this because she is unsure of how this will affect Judy. The mother is sharing the information with you because she knows Judy is close to you and the mother wants you to be aware of what is occurring in Judy's life. Role-play your conversation with Judy's mother.

Scenario #6

You are a teacher. A guidance counselor approaches you and states he saw John's father coming out of a known gay bar late last Saturday night, arm in arm with another man. Role-play a dialogue between you and the guidance counselor. Discuss how you might want to handle this situation with John.

Handout 9.3. Permission is granted to photocopy for classroom use.

Activity 9.4
EDUCATORS WORKING WITH GAY
AND LESBIAN PARENTS

Objective: To present some basic information regarding students and their homosexual parents
Estimated Time: 30 to 35 minutes
Materials Needed: Handout 9.4: Guidelines for Educators Working with Students Who Have Gay or Lesbian Parents (one copy for each participant)

Directions for Facilitators

1. Using the Background Information, make a presentation to the entire group regarding the adjustment students must make if their parents are homosexual.
2. Following the presentation, distribute Handout 9.4 (one copy to each participant).
3. Discuss each item in the handout and entertain any discussion that may arise from each item.

BACKGROUND INFORMATION

According to researchers, between one and three million gay men are natural fathers (Bozett, 1987) and 6 million (Schulenberg, 1985) to 14 million (Peterson, 1984) children have gay or lesbian parents. Consequently, there is a strong likelihood that a fair number of students in a given school has one or more gay or lesbian parents. Because parents may be in various stages of adjusting to their own sexual issues when their child discovers his or her parent is homosexual, teachers can expect a continuum of responses from these students and their parents. Some of the responses may include the following:

1. The student not wanting to spend any time with the parent who is gay or lesbian.
2. The student not wanting his or her friends to know he or she has a gay or lesbian parent.
3. The student engaging in atypical behavior (e.g., withdrawing, being aggressive, performing poorly in his/her courses, etc.).
4. The student being in denial that anything is different about the family composition.
5. The student wanting to talk about his or her family situation with others, but not knowing how to react to peer responses.
6. The student exhibiting a lackadaisical attitude and seeming to adapt rather well.

Parents do not always know how to react to the knowledge that they themselves are gay or that their spouse is gay. In addition to their own adjustment, they are not sure what the best approach may be to take with their children. Consequently, many parents do not discuss the issue until it comes up unexpectedly, and when they do discuss it they may not be fully prepared to handle their child's questions or they may not allow their child to share his or her feelings with them. As a result, all family members are affected and, generally, all of them go through a significant period of adjustment. Discussing these issues is usually difficult for all parties involved and educators need to be sensitive in this area. Many times educators are even unaware that this may be an issue and are unprepared when this topic comes up for discussion. Educators may want to sensitize themselves for dealing with these issues by addressing the following issues within themselves:

1. How are you perceived by others? Judgmental? Accepting? Threatening? Intimidating? Confrontational?
2. Can you identify your prejudices? How are your actions and attitudes toward students affected by these prejudices?

3. Do any of your attitudes and beliefs in working with your students need to be modified?
4. How do you feel about homosexuality? Do you feel you would have difficulty in assisting students to handle and adjust to parental homosexuality?
5. Is there someone in your family who is gay or lesbian? How do you feel about this?
6. How do you think you would respond if your parent or sibling identified himself/herself as gay or lesbian?
7. How would you feel if your best friend were gay or lesbian?
8. What is your reaction to hostile humor such as gay and lesbian jokes?
9. What are the limits of confidentiality?

References

Bozett, F. W. (Ed.). (1987). *Gay and lesbian parents.* New York: Praeger.

Peterson, N. (1984, April 30). Coming to terms with gay parents. *USA Today*, p. 30.

Schulenberg, J. A. (1985). *Gay parenting: A complete guide for gay men and lesbians with children.* Garden City, NY: Anchor Books.

Background Information for Activity 9.4.   Permission is granted to photocopy for classroom use.

Handout 9.4
GUIDELINES FOR EDUCATORS WORKING WITH STUDENTS WHO HAVE GAY OR LESBIAN PARENTS

Directions for Participants

1. Listen as the facilitator reads each of the statements below.
2. Enter into the discussion of each guideline.

1. Try to be nonjudgmental in your approach to others. If you have prejudices and biases, be aware of them and recognize how they might affect your work with others.
2. Maintain confidentiality. If you are trusted with privileged information, respect it and do not share it with others.
3. Be supportive. Send messages to others that you are a person who accepts all kinds of differences. There are many family constellations and having a gay or lesbian parent is one of those family patterns.
4. Identify the student and family's understanding of the situation in as simplistic a manner as possible. Sometimes identifying the difficulties is the first step toward greater understanding and acceptance. Help to foster communication among family members if at all possible.
5. Assist in the development of a support group within the school system or your community to help bring together students who may be in the same situation. Having an outlet for discussion may help students feel less isolated or alone.
6. Know the referral sources in the community. Don't hesitate to refer the family or student to a professional or support group that can help them deal with their feelings.

7. Be informed and serve as a resource person. Let others know that you have access to literature or information that can help them learn to handle their feelings and concerns. Make colleagues aware of the resources available for all types of questions and situations.

Handout 9.4.   Permission is granted to photocopy for classroom use.

INDIVIDUAL ACTION PLANS

This section represents the raison d'être for the workshop. A training workshop is a vehicle for learning, and learning implies change—a change in knowledge base, attitude, and/or behavior. Changing one's own behavior and influencing the behavior of others as a result of the workshop experience are not easy tasks. Several forces can work to destroy a workshop participant's good intentions (e.g., the return to the usual on-the-job pressures, possible lack of support from those in charge, the disappearance of support from the workshop participants and facilitators, or the absence of opportunities to communicate with the people who shared the workshop experience).

Specific individual action plans (personal commitments to apply new behavior on the job) can convert the training to concrete and realistic application in the workplace or educational setting. Activity 10.1: Analysis of Change familiarizes participants with the driving forces and the restraining forces that support or resist change in the status quo (e.g., invisibility and silence regarding sexual orientation among gays and lesbians). Activity 10.2: Development of Participants' Individual Action Plans provides the opportunity for participants to develop their individual action plans for change on the job as a result of the workshop experience. After the individual action plans have been developed, each participant will share his or her plan with a partner to reinforce the commitment and receive feedback. The action plans are considered "contracts" for change.

Activity 10.1
ANALYSIS OF CHANGE

Objective: To create an awareness of forces that support and resist change in the status quo associated with gays and lesbians in educational and workplace settings
Estimated Time: 50 to 55 minutes
Materials Needed: Easel, chart paper, and marker for facilitators; Handout 10.1 (Part A): Analysis of Change; Handout 10.1 (Part B): Workshop Facilitators' List of Possibilities: Analysis of Change (one copy of each for each group)

Directions for Facilitators

1. Organize participants in groups of four or six.
2. Read the following to participants. "Whenever change is instigated with respect to the status quo, there are usually forces that support the change and forces that resist the change. These opposing forces influence the rate of speed with which a change occurs; some changes take place rapidly, others slowly. Example of rapid change: transmission and storage of information with the advent of computers. Example of slow change: the structure of the American family, from traditional nuclear families to alternative families."
3. Distribute one copy of Handout 10.1 (Part A) to each group and instruct them to follow the directions on the handout. (Allow approximately 20 to 25 minutes for completion of the activity).
4. Initiate a general discussion by calling on each group to contribute one or two "forces supporting the status quo." Chart eight or ten of their contributions, then do the same for the "forces resisting the status quo." [Compare the chart lists with Handout 10.1 (Part B).]
5. Distribute Handout 10.1 (Part B) (one copy to each group) for participants to compare with their responses on Handout 10.1 (Part A).
6. Facilitate any questions they may have.

Handout 10.1 (Part A)
ANALYSIS OF CHANGE

Directions for Participants

1. Select a member of the group to facilitate the activity.
2. Through discussion of the various supporting and resisting forces for the status quo, come to a consensus within the group and record below those that are clearly identified.
3. When the workshop facilitator calls for contributions from each group, have your group facilitator respond for your group.

In this instance, the status quo refers to gays' and lesbians' invisibility and silence concerning their sexual orientation in educational and workplace settings.

Forces Supporting the Status Quo	Forces Resisting the Status Quo
1.	1.
2.	2.
3.	3.
4.	4.
5.	5.
6.	6.
7.	7.
8.	8.
9.	9.
10.	10.

Handout 10.1 (Part A). Permission is granted to photocopy for classroom use.

Handout 10.1 (Part B)
WORKSHOP FACILITATORS' LIST OF POSSIBILITIES:
ANALYSIS OF CHANGE

Directions for Participants

1. Compare your group's list from Handout 10.1 (Part A) with the list below.
2. Enter into a discussion with the larger group regarding the forces.

Forces Supporting the Status Quo	Forces Resisting the Status
1. Homophobia	1. Stated antidiscrimination policies of some educational institutions and major corporations
2. Heterosexism	
3. Fear	
4. Religious views	
5. Ignorance about gays and lesbians	2. Local, state, and federal antidiscrimination policies and laws
6. Political conservatism	
7. Stereotyping	3. Education
8. Myths regarding gays and lesbians	4. Positive gay/lesbian role models
9. Generalizing	5. Political philosophies (e.g., liberalism, civil rights activism)
10. Values	
	6. Constitutional law
	7. Economic interests (e.g., profit motive)
	8. Values
	9. Media
	10. Religious institutions

Handout 10.1 (Part B).   Permission is granted to photocopy for classroom use.

Activity 10.2
DEVELOPMENT OF PARTICIPANTS'
INDIVIDUAL ACTION PLANS

Objective: To have each participant apply change analysis and write an individual action plan for change in the status quo regarding gays and lesbians in his or her educational or workplace setting

Estimated Time: 30 to 40 minutes

Materials Needed: Handout 10.2: Individual Action Plan for Change in the Educational or Workplace Setting (one copy for each participant)

Directions for Facilitators

1. Read the activity objective to participants.
2. Distribute Handout 10.2 to all participants and ask them to follow the directions on the handout. (Allow approximately 20 to 25 minutes for this part of the activity.)
3. When the activity has been completed, ask each participant to share his or her action plan with a partner for reinforcement and augmented commitment.
4. When all participants have shared their action plans with a partner, ask for two volunteers to share their action plans with the entire workshop group.

Note: Postworkshop monitoring of individual action plans is ideal, but would depend on the facilitators' workplace/educational setting connections with the workshop participants. If monitoring is feasible, one of the following procedures may be applied:

a. Collect the individual action plans and mail them back to the participants in two or three weeks as a reminder of their workshop commitment.
b. Thirty days after the workshop mail each participant a reinforcing note concerning his or her individual action plan.
c. Ask each participant to choose another person in the workshop to keep in touch with concerning his or her action plan.
d. After the workshop, send participants a short questionnaire concerning accomplishment of the action plan and ask them to return the questionnaire to you.

Handout 10.2
INDIVIDUAL ACTION PLAN FOR CHANGE IN THE
EDUCATIONAL OR WORKPLACE SETTING

Directions for Participants

Develop your plan of action by completing the four items below. (It should take
approximately 20 to 25 minutes to complete this activity.)

1. WHAT I HOPE TO ACCOMPLISH to facilitate positive
   change in my educational/workplace setting:
   a. _____
   b. _____
   c. _____
   d. _____
   e. _____

2. The SUPPORTING FORCES in my educational/work-
   place settings are:
   a. _____
   b. _____
   c. _____
   d. _____
   e. _____

3. The RESISTING FORCES in my educational/work-
   place setting are:
   a. _____
   b. _____
   c. _____
   d. _____
   e. _____

4. My INDIVIDUAL PLAN OF ACTION to facilitate the changes listed in #1 above:

   a. _____

   b. _____

   c. _____

   d. _____

   e. _____

Handout 10.2. Permission is granted to photocopy for classroom use.

REPLICATING THE WORKSHOP TRAINING FOR COLLEAGUES IN EDUCATIONAL AND WORKPLACE SETTINGS

This workshop, when competently facilitated, has the potential to change attitudes through dispelling myths, dissipating ignorance, breaking down stereotypes, and providing participants with accurate information concerning the gay and lesbian population.

Society benefits when an oppressed segment of the population is freed and encouraged to develop its potential and talents in an atmosphere of acceptance; the result is an enriched society. Commitment and education concerning the gay and lesbian population is necessary for understanding, reduction of prejudice, and positive change. Workshop participants have the opportunity to contribute to positive change by assuming a leadership role, motivating others, and replicating the training for their colleagues in educational and workplace settings.

The goal of the activities in this section is to focus participants' attention on the essential facilitator competencies and the preparation required for replicating the training they have experienced in the workshop. Participants may have varying degrees of skills in leading workshops; some may be competent trainers, whereas others may have only some experience or be totally inexperienced but willing to make the commitment to prepare themselves for the job. Included in this section is a list of books that may be helpful to participants who wish to read about training design and methods of delivery.

Activity 11.1
CHARACTERISTICS OF COMPETENT FACILITATORS

Objective: To have participants develop a list of workshop facilitator competencies necessary for training others
Estimated Time: 40 to 45 minutes
Materials Needed: Chart paper, markers, and masking tape (for each of the small groups); chart pad, easel, and markers for facilitators

Directions for Facilitators

1. Organize participants into groups of six and ask each group to select a leader.
2. Distribute chart paper, markers, and masking tape to each group.
3. Instruct each group to brainstorm a list of facilitator competencies they believe are necessary to train a group of professionals. Ask them to list the competencies on the chart paper. (Allow approximately 20 minutes for this part of the activity.)
4. When all groups have completed the lists, ask each leader to post the list and share the competencies with the entire workshop group.
5. After all leaders have presented, the facilitators should compile and chart a master list, integrating competencies from participants' lists and the list provided below:

- Have a strong knowledge base in the content area in which they train
- Are familiar with techniques for training adult learners
- Have a sophisticated sense of humor
- Are active listeners and are nonjudgmental
- Are democratic leaders
- Understand and assume the role of a facilitator of learning
- Respect the attitudes and ideas of all participants
- Are sensitive to the needs of individual learners
- Have expertise in handling participants who verbally attack the attitudes and ideas of fellow participants
- Are task oriented and well prepared to implement the workshop agenda
- Work to keep all participants involved and on task
- Use a variety of activities relative to the content objectives
- Provide icebreakers, short energizers, team-building exercises, and brief breaks from the agenda

Activity 11.2
PREPARING FOR TRAINING

Objective: To focus participants' attention on various decisions that must be made in the preparation for a workshop on gay and lesbian issues

Estimated Time: 30 to 35 minutes

Materials Needed: Paper and pencils for participants; Handout 11.2: A Checklist for Replicating the Workshop Training for Professionals Who Work with Gay and Lesbian Individuals (one for each participant); six 3 × 5 cards prepared in advance by facilitators (see Directions for Facilitators)

Directions for Facilitators

1. Organize participants into six groups
2. Distribute the six prepared 3 × 5 cards, one to each group. Each card should bear one question from the following list:

   Which criteria should be used in selecting a training facility for a workshop?

   In addition to content items, what other items should be listed on a workshop agenda?

   What are the advantages to soliciting *volunteer* participants to attend a workshop dealing with gay and lesbian issues?

   What are the advantages to *requiring* participants to attend a workshop dealing with gay and lesbian issues?

   List five or six workshop objectives for training educators in gay and lesbian issues.

   List five or six workshop objectives for training corporate and other workplace professionals in gay and lesbian issues.

3. Instruct the groups to collaborate and write their answer to the assigned questions. (Allow 10 to 15 minutes to complete this part of the activity.)
4. When participants have finished, call on each group to share its question and answer with all workshop participants. (Facilitate discussion.)
5. Distribute Handout 11.2 (one copy for each participant).
6. Facilitate further discussion based on the handout.

Handout 11.2
CHECKLIST FOR REPLICATING TRAINING FOR PROFESSIONALS WHO WORK WITH GAY AND LESBIAN INDIVIDUALS

Directions for Participants

1. Read the following list.
2. Add to the list if you know of any other items.
3. Keep the list for your use.

- Make or obtain an executive/administrative decision to replicate training and set a time and date.
- Choose facilitators who are experienced in training adults and are knowledgeable in the content.
- Decide if training will be voluntary or mandated.
- Solicit participants (no more than 30).
- Select a training site.
- Order training manual (*Training for Professionals Who Work with Gays and Lesbians in Educational and Workplace Settings*) from Accelerated Development, 1900 Frost Rd., Suite 101, Bristol, PA 19007-1598; 1-800-821-8312.
- Select the sections and activities to be included in the workshop, based on time constraints and objectives to be achieved for determined participants.
- Order supportive materials (videotapes, publications, etc.) from resources listed in the back of the training manual.
- Arrange for in-house audio–visual equipment and materials.
- Develop an agenda.

- Duplicate agenda and necessary handouts for participants.
- Obtain and prepare other materials called for in the chosen activities.
- Prepare any necessary registration materials, including name tags for participants and facilitators.
- Notify participants of date, time, and site for the workshop.
- Arrange for refreshments for workshop breaks.
- Rehearse . . . rehearse . . . rehearse for delivery of the workshop.

Recommended Reading

Davis, L., & McCallon, E. (1974). *Planning, conducting and evaluating workshops.* Austin, TX: Learning Concepts.

Effington, J. (1989). *The winning trainer.* Houston, TX: Gulf Publishing.

McLagan, P. (1978). *Helping others learn: Designing programs for adults.* Reading, MA: Addison-Wesley.

Silberman, M. (1990). *Active training: Handbook of techniques, designs, case examples and tips.* New York: Lexington Books.

Tracey, W. (1992). *Designing training and development systems.* New York: AMACOM (Division of American Management Association).

Handout 11.2.   Permission is granted to photocopy for classroom use.

REVIEW OF RESOURCES

This section acquaints the facilitators and participants with the following resources related to the content of the workshop:

Books
Periodicals
Brochures, handbooks, resource guides, and curriculum materials
Audiotapes
Videotapes
Organizations
Hotlines

Through these resources, workshop participants and facilitators can broaden their knowledge of the subject matter and select various resources to enhance the planning and delivery of training.

BOOKS

Abelove, H., Barale, M. A., & Halperin, D. (1993). *The lesbian and gay studies reader*. New York: Routledge.

Alpert, H. (1988). *We are everywhere: Writings by and about lesbian parents*. Marshall, MN: Crossing Press.

Altman, D. (1983). *The homosexualization of America: The Americanization of the homosexual*. Boston: Beacon Press.

Alyson, S. (Ed.). (1991). *Young, gay, & proud!* Boston: Alyson.

Andrews, N. (1994). *Family: A portrait of gay and lesbian America.* New York: HarperCollins.

Baker, D. B., Strubs, S., & Henning, B. (1995). *Cracking the corporate closet.* New York: HarperCollins.

Balka, C., & Rose, A. (Eds.). (1991). *Twice blessed: On being lesbian or gay and Jewish.* Boston: Beacon Press.

Barrett, M. B. (1990). *Invisible lives: The truth about millions of women-loving women.* New York: Perennial Lib.

Bawer, B. (1993). *A place at the table: The gay individual in American society.* New York: Poseidon Press.

Bell, A. P., & Weinberg, M. S. (1978). *Homosexualities: A study of diversity among men and women.* New York: Simon & Schuster.

Bell, A. P., Weinberg, M. S., & Hammersmith, S. K. (1981). *Sexual preference: Its development in men and women.* Bloomington, IN: Indiana University Press.

Benkov, L. (1994). *Reinventing the family.* New York: Crown Publishers.

Berger, R. M. (1982). *Gay and gray: The older homosexual man.* Urbana, IL: University of Illinois Press.

Bérubé, A. (1990). *Coming out under fire: The history of gay men and women in World War Two.* New York: Free Press.

Berzon, B. (Ed.). (1992). *Positively gay: New approaches to gay and lesbian life.* Berkeley, CA: Celestial Arts.

Blumenfeld, W. J. (Ed.). (1992). *Homophobia: How we all pay the price.* Boston: Beacon Press.

Blumenfeld, W. J., & Raymond, D. (1993). *Looking at gay and lesbian life* (2nd ed.). Boston: Beacon Press.

Borhek, M. V. (1984). *My son Eric.* Cleveland, OH: Pilgrim Press.

Brohek, M. V. (1993). *Coming out to parents.* Cleveland, OH: Pilgrim Press.

Bozett, F. W. (Ed.). (1987). *Gay and lesbian parents.* New York: Praeger.

Bozett, F. W., & Sussman, M. B. (Eds.). (1990). *Homosexuality and family relations.* Binghamton, NY: Haworth Press.

Brown, H. (1989). *Familiar faces, hidden lives.* Orlando, FL: Harcourt, Brace, Jovanovich.

Buxton, A. P. (1994). *The coming-out crisis for straight spouses and families.* New York: John Wiley & Sons.

Clark, D. (1992). *The new loving someone gay.* Berkeley, CA: Celestial Arts.

Cohen, S., & Cohen, D. (1992). *When someone you know is gay.* New York: Dell.

Comstock, G. (1991). *Violence against lesbians and gay men.* New York: Columbian University Press.

Cowan, T. D. (1988). *Gay men and women who enriched the world.* New Canaan, CT: Mulvey Books.

Curtis, W. (Ed.). (1988). *Revelations: A collection of gay male coming out stories.* Boston: Alyson.

Damron, B. (1993). *The 29th edition of Bob Damron's address book.* San Francisco: Author.

Davis, L., & McCallon, E. (1974). *Planning, conducting and evaluating workshops.* Austin, TX: Learning Concepts.

DeCecco, J. (Ed.). (1987). *Gay relationships.* New York: Harrington Park Press.

DeCrescenzo, T. (Ed.). (1994). *Helping gay and lesbian youth: New policies, new programs, new practices.* New York: Harrington Park Press.

D'Emilio, J. (1985). *Bashers, baiters and bigots: Homophobia in American society.* New York: Harrington Park Press.

Denman, R. M. (1990). *Let my people in: A lesbian minister tells of her struggles to live openly and maintain her ministry.* New York: Morrow.

Dew, R. F. (1994). *The family heart: A memoir of when our son came out.* New York: Addison-Wesley.

Doaghe, R. E. (1989). *Common sons.* Austin, TX: Edward William.

Duberman, M. (1993). *Stonewall.* New York: Dutton.

Dyer, K. (1990). *Gays in uniform.* Boston: Alyson.

Effington, J. (1989). *The winning trainer.* Houston, TX: Gulf Publishing.

Eichberg, R. (1991). *Coming out: An act of love.* New York: Plume.

Fairchild, B., & Hayward, N. (1989). *Now that you know: What every parent should know about homosexuality.* San Diego: Harcourt, Brace, Jovanovich.

Freud, S. (1953). Three essays on the theory of sexuality. In J. Strachey (Ed. and Trans.), *The standard edition of the complete psychological works of Sigmund Freud* (Vol. 7, pp. 125–245). London: Hogarth Press. (Original work published 1901)

Freud, S. (1963). Certain neurotic mechanisms. In *Sexuality and the psychology of love* (pp. 150–160). New York: Collier.

Fricke, A. (1981). *Reflections of a rock lobster: A story about growing up gay.* Boston: Alyson.

Friskopp, A., & Silverstein, S. (1995). *Straight jobs, gay lives.* New York: Scribner.

Gay American Indians. (1988). *Living the spirit: A gay American Indian anthology.* New York: St. Martin's Press.

Gonsiorek, J., & Weinrich, J. (1991). *Homosexuality: Research implications for public policy.* New bury Park, CA: Sage.

Green, R. (1987). *The "sissy boy syndrome" and the development of homosexuality.* New Haven, CT: Yale University Press.

Griffin, C., & Wirth, M. A. (1990). *Beyond acceptance.* New York: St. Martin's Press.

Hanckel, F., & Cunningham, J. (1979). *A way of love, a way of life: A young person's introduction to what it means to be gay.* New York: Lothrop, Lee & Shepard.

Harbeck, K. M. (Ed.). (1992). *Coming out of the classroom closet: Gay and lesbian students, teachers and curricula.* New York: Harrington Park Press.

Harry, J., & DeVall, W. (1978). *The social organization of gay males.* New York: Praeger.

Herdt, G. (Ed.). (1989). *Gay and lesbian youth.* New York: Harrington Park Press.

Herdt, G., & Boxer, A. (1993). *Children of horizons: How gay and lesbian teens are leading a new way out of the closet.* Boston: Beacon Press.

Herek, G. (1984). *Beyond "homophobia": A social psychological perspective on attitudes toward lesbians and gay men.* Binghamton, NY: Haworth Press.

Herek, G. M., & Berrill, K. T. (1992). *Hate crimes: Confronting violence against lesbians and gay men.* Newbury Park, CA: Sage.

Heron, A. (Ed.). (1983). *One teenager in ten.* Boston: Alyson.

Heron, A. (Ed.). (1994). *Two teenagers in twenty: Writings by gay and lesbian youth.* Boston: Alyson.

Hippler, M. (1989). *Matlovich: The good soldier.* Boston: Alyson.

Holmes, S. (Ed.). (1994). *Testimonies: A collection of lesbian coming out stories.* Boston: Alyson.

Holobaugh, J., & Hale, K. (1992). *Torn allegiances: The story of a gay cadet.* Boston: Alyson.

Hunter, N. D., Michaelson, S. E., & Stoddard, T. B. (1992). *The rights of lesbians and gay men: The basic ACLU guide to a gay person's rights.* Carbondale, IL: Southern Illinois University Press.

Hutchins, L., & Kaahumanu, L. (Eds.). (1991). *Bi any other name: Bisexual people speak out.* Boston: Alyson.

Isay, R. (1989). *Being homosexual: Gay men and their development*. New York: Farrar, Straus & Giroux.

Jennings, K. (Ed.). (1994). *Becoming visible: A reader in gay and lesbian history for high school and college students*. Boston: Alyson.

Jennings, K. (Ed.). (1994). *One teacher in ten: Lesbian and gay educators tell their stories*. Boston: Alyson.

Kagan, J., & Moss, H. A. (1962). *Birth to maturity*. New York: Wiley.

Kanter, R. (1993). *Men and women of the corporation*. New York: Basic Books.

Kenan, R. (1994). *James Baldwin*. New York: Chelsea House.

Khayatt, M. D. (1992). *Lesbian teachers: An invisible presence*. Albany, NY: State University of New York Press.

Kinsey, A. C., Pomeroy, W. B., & Martin, C. E. (1948). *Sexual behavior in the human male*. Philadelphia: W.B. Saunders.

Kinsey, A. C., Pomeroy, W., Martin, C. E., & Gebhard, R. (1953). *Sexual behavior in the human female*. Philadelphia: W.B. Saunders.

Kopay, D., & Young, P. (1988). *The David Kopay story*. New York: Donald I. Fine, Inc.

Leinen, S. (1993). *Gay cops*. New Brunswick, NJ: Rutgers University Press.

Leming, D. (1994). *James Baldwin*. New York: Knopf.

Le Vay, S., & Nonas, E. (1995). *City of friends: A portrait of the gay and lesbian community in America*. Cambridge, MA: MIT Press.

Lewes, K. (1988). *The psychoanalytic theory of male homosexuality*. New York: Simon & Schuster.

Likosky, S. (Ed.). (1992). *Coming out: An anthology of international gay and lesbian writings*. New York: Pantheon Books.

Louganis, G., with Eric Marcus. (1995). *Breaking the surface*. New York: Random House.

MacPike, L. (Ed.). (1989). *There's something I've been meaning to tell you.* Tallahassee, FL: Naiad Press.

Marcus, E. (1992). *Making history: The struggle for gay and lesbian equal rights.* New York: HarperCollins.

Marcus, E. (1993). *Is it a choice?* New York: HarperCollins.

Martin, A. (1993). *The lesbian and gay parenting handbook: Creating and raising our families.* New York: HarperCollins.

Mayer, M. (1993). *Gay, lesbian and heterosexual teachers: An investigation of acceptance of self, acceptance of others, affectional and lifestyle orientation: Their rightful places.* Lewiston, NY: The Edwin Mellen Press.

McConnell-Celi, S. (1993). *The 21st challenge: Lesbians and gays in education.* Red Bank, NJ: Lavender Crystal Press.

McLagan, P. (1978). *Helping others learn: Designing programs for adults.* Reading, MA: Addison-Wesley.

McNaught, B. (1989). *On being gay.* New York: St. Martin's Press.

McNaught, B. (1993). *Gay issues in the workplace.* New York: St. Martin's Press.

Mickens, E. (1994). *The 100 best companies for gay men and lesbians.* New York: Pocketbooks.

Miller, A. (1984). *Thou shalt not be aware: Society's betrayal of the child.* New York: Farrar, Straus & Giroux.

Mohr, R. D. (1988). *Gays/justice: A study of ethics, society and law.* New York: Columbia University Press.

Mohr, R. D. (1994). *A more perfect union: Why straight America must stand up for gay rights.* Boston: Beacon.

Monette, P. (1992). *Becoming a man: Half a life's story.* New York: Harcourt, Brace, Jovanovich.

Morales, A. L. (1986). *Getting home alive.* Ithaca, NY: Firebrand Books.

Morse, C., & Larkin, J. (Eds.). (1988). *Gay and lesbian poetry of our time: An anthology.* New York: St. Martin's Press.

Muller, A. (1987). *Parents matter.* Tallahassee, FL: Naiad Press.

Nardi, P. M., Sanders, D., & Marmor, J. (1994). *Growing up before Stonewall.* New York: Routledge.

Nava, M., & Dawidoff, R. (1994). *Created equal: Why gay rights matter to America.* New York: St. Martin's Press.

O'Brien, S. (1995). *Lives of notable gays and lesbians: Willa Cather.* New York: Chelsea House.

Overlooked Opinions. (1992, January). *The gay market.* Chicago: Author.

Pallone, D., & Steinberg, A. (1991). *Behind the mask: My double life in baseball.* New York: Dutton.

Paul, W., Weinrich, J. D., Gonsiorek, J. C., & Hotvedt, M. E. (Eds.). (1982). *Homosexuality: Social, psychological and biological issues.* Beverly Hills, CA: Sage.

Peck, S. (1995). *All American boy: A memoir.* New York: Scribner.

Penelope, J., & Wolfe, S. J. (Eds.). (1993). *Lesbian culture: Anthology.* Freedom, CA: Crossing Press.

Peplau, L. A. (1983/1984). What homosexuals want. In O. Pocs (Ed.), *Human sexuality* (pp. 201–207). Guilford, CT: Dushkin Publishing.

Pharr, S. (1988). *Homophobia: A weapon of sexism.* Inverness, CA: Chardon Press.

Plant, R. (1986). *The pink triangle: The Nazi war against homosexuals.* New York: Holt.

Preston, J. (Ed.). (1994). *A member of the family.* New York: Plume.

Price, D., & Murdoch, J. (1995). *And say hi to Joyce.* New York: Doubleday.

Rafkin, L. (Ed.). (1987) *Different daughters: A book by mothers of lesbians.* Pittsburgh, PA: Cleis Press.

Rafkin, L. (Ed.). (1990). *Different mothers: Sons and daughters of lesbians talk about their lives.* Pittsburgh, PA: Cleis Press.

Ramos, J. (Ed.). (1987). *Compañeras. Latina lesbians: An anthology.* New York: Latina Lesbian History Project.

Rasi, R., & Rodriguez-Noques, L. (Eds.). (1995). *Out in the workplace: The pleasures and perils of coming out on the job.* Los Angeles: Alyson.

Ratti, R. (Ed.). (1993). *A lotus of another color: An unfolding of the South Asian gay and lesbian experience.* Boston: Alyson.

Reid, J. (1993). *The best little boy in the world: The true and moving story of coming to terms with being gay.* New York: Ballantine.

Remafedi, G. *Death by denial.* (1994). Boston: Alyson.

Reynolds, M. (Ed.). (1993). *The Penguin book of lesbian short stories.* New York: Viking.

Rofes, E. (1985). *Socrates, Plato, and guys like me: Confessions of a gay schoolteacher.* Los Angeles: Alyson.

Roscoe, W. (1989). *Living the spirit: A gay native American anthology.* New York: St. Martin's Press.

Rubenstein, W. B. (Ed.). (1993). *Lesbians, gay men and the law.* New York: The New Press.

Saghir, M., & Robbins, E. (1973). *Male and female homosexuality: A comprehensive investigation.* Baltimore: Williams & Wilkins.

Savin-Williams, R. C. (1990). *Gay and lesbian youth: Expressions of identity.* New York: Hemisphere.

Schulenburg, J. (1985). *Gay parenting: A complete guide for gay men and lesbians with children.* Garden City, NY: Anchor Books.

Schulman, S. (1994). *My American history: Lesbian and gay life during the Reagan/Bush years.* New York: Routhledge.

Sears, J. T. (1991). *Growing up gay in the South: Race, gender and journeys of the spirit.* New York: Haworth Press.

Sherman, P., & Bernstein, S. (Eds.). (1994). *Uncommon heroes: A celebration of heroes and role models for gay and lesbian Americans*. New York: Fletcher Press.

Sherrill, J.-M., & Hardesty, C. A. (1994). *The gay, lesbian and bisexual students' guide to colleges, universities, and graduate schools*. New York: NYU Press.

Shilts, R. (1982). *The mayor of Castro Street: The life and times of Harvey Milk*. New York: St. Martin's Press.

Shilts, R. (1987). *And the band played on: People, politics, and the AIDS epidemic*. New York: St. Martin's Press.

Shilts, R. (Ed.). (1992). *Sexuality and the curriculum*. New York: Columbia University Press.

Shilts, R. (1993). *Conduct unbecoming: Gays and lesbians in the U.S. military*. New York: St. Martin's Press.

Siegel, S., & Lowe, E., Jr. (1994). *Uncharted lives: The psychological journey of gay men*. New York: Dutton.

Silberman, M. (1990). *Active training: Handbook of techniques, designs, case example and tips*. New York: Lexington Books.

Singer, B. L. (1994). *Growing up lesbian*. New York: The New Press.

Singer, B. L., & Deschamps, D. (Eds.). (1994). *Gay and lesbian stats: A pocket guide of facts and figures*. New York: The New Press.

Skidelsky, R. (1986). *John Maynard Keynes: Hopes betrayed, 1883–1920*. New York: Viking.

Spence, J., & Helmreich, R. (1978). *Masculinity and femininity: Their psychological dimensions, correlates, and antecedents*. Austin: University of Texas Press.

Spoto, D. (1985). *The kindness of strangers: The life of Tennessee Williams*. Boston: Little, Brown.

Steffan, J. (1993). *Honor bound*. New York: Avon.

Thompson, W. (1995). *The price of achievement: Coming out in the Reagan days*. New York: Cassell.

Toder, N. (1991). *Choices*. Boston: Alyson.

Tracey, W. (1992). *Designing training and development systems*. New York: AMACOM (Division of American Management Association).

Tripp, C. A. (1987). *The homosexual matrix* (2nd ed.). New York: Meridian.

Vaid, U. (1995). *Virtual equality: The mainstreaming of gay and lesbian liberation*. New York: Anchor Books.

Wakeling, L., & Bradstock, M. (Eds.). (1995). *Beyond blood: Writings on the lesbian and gay family*. Sydney, Australia: Black Wattle Press.

Walters, A. L. (1992). *Talking Indian: Reflections on survival and writing*. Ithaca, NY: Firebrand Books.

Webster, H. (1991). *Family secrets: How telling and not telling affects our children, our relationships and our lives*. New York: Addison-Wesley.

Weinberg, M. S., Williams, C. J., & Pryor, D. W. (1994). *Dual attraction: Understanding bisexuality*. New York: Oxford University Press.

Weinrich, J. D. (1987). *Sexual landscapes: Why we are what we are, why we love whom we love*. New York: Scribner.

Weston, K. (1991). *Families we choose: Lesbians, gays, kinship*. New York: Columbia University Press.

White, M. (1994). *Stranger at the gate: To be gay and Christian in America*. New York: Simon & Schuster.

Whitlock, K. (1989). *Bridges of respect: Creating support for lesbian and gay youth*. Philadelphia: American Friends Service Committee.

Williams, W. (1987). *The spirit and the flesh: Sexual diversity in American Indian culture*. New York: Harper & Row.

Woodman, N. J. (Ed.). (1992). *Lesbian and gay lifestyles: A guide for counseling and education*. New York: Irvington.

Woods, J. D., & Lucas, J. H. (1993). *The corporate closet: The professional lives of gay men in America*. New York: The Free Press.

Woog, D. (1995). *School's out: The impact of gay and lesbian issues on America's schools.* Boston: Alyson.

Zanotti, B. (Ed.). (1986). *A faith of one's own: Explorations by Catholic lesbians.* Marshall, MN: Crossing Press.

PERIODICALS

Acanfora v. Board of Education of Montgomery County, 359 F. Supp. 846 (District Court, Montgomery Country, MD, 1974).

Allen, L. S., Hines, M., Shryne, J. E., & Gorski, R. A. (1986). Two sexually dimorphic cell groups in the human brain. *Endrocrinolgy* (Suppl.), *118*, 633.

American Psychological Association. (1975). Proceedings of the American Psychological Association for the year 1974. *American Psychologist, 30*, 620–651.

Anderson, D. (1987). Family and peer relations of gay adolescents. *Adolescent Psychiatry, 14*, 165–178.

Angier, N. (1993, March 12). Study suggests strong genetic role in lesbianism. *New York Times*, p. A8 (N), p. A11 (L).

Angier, N. (1993, July 18). Research on sex orientation doesn't neatly fit the mold. *New York Times*, p. 13.

Association for Supervision & Curriculum Development (ASCD). (1992, March). At-risk kids schools ignore. *Executive Educator* (Newsletter), *14*(3), 28–31.

Association for Supervision & Curriculum Development. (1990). Student sexual orientation. *Resolutions 1990* [Flyer]. Alexandria, VA: Author.

Attempts to cure homosexuality could mean litigation. (1994, June 13). *Mental Health Weekly, 4*(23), 1–2.

Bailey, J. M. (1993). Heritable factors influence sexual orientation in women. *Archives of General Psychiatry, 50*, 217–223.

Bailey, J. M., & Pillard, R. A. (1991, December). Genetic study of male sexual orientation. *Archives of General Psychiatry, 48*, 1089–1096.

Bem, S. (1974). The measurement of psychological androgyny. *Journal of Consulting & Counseling Psychology, 42*, 155–162.

Bem, S. (1975). Sex-role adaptability: One consequence of psychological androgyny. *Journal of Personality & Social Psychology, 31*, 634–643.

Berger, G., Hank, L., Rauzi, T., & Simkins, L. (1987). Detection of sexual orientation by heterosexuals and homosexuals. *Journal of Homosexuality, 13*(4), 83–100.

Berkhan, W. (1990). *Guide to curriculum planning in suicide prevention.* Madison, WI: Wisconsin Department of Public Instruction.

Bernstein, R. A. (1988, February 24). My daughter is a lesbian. *New York Times*, p. A27.

Bidwell, R. J. (1988). The gay and lesbian teen: A case of denied adolescence. *Journal of Pediatric Health Care, 2*, 3–8.

Block, J. H. (1973). Conceptions of sex role: Some cross-cultural and longitudinal perspectives. *American Psychologist, 28*, 512–526.

Boxer, A. M., & Cohler, B. J. (1989). The life course of gay and lesbian youth: An immodest proposal for the study of lives. *Journal of Homosexuality, 17*, 315–355.

Bozett, F. W. (1980). Gay fathers: How and why they disclose their homosexuality to their children. *Family Relations: Journal of Applied Family & Child Studies, 29*, 173–179.

Bozett, F. W. (1981). Gay fathers: Identity conflict resolution through integrative sanctioning. *Alternative Lifestyles, 4*, 90–107.

Bozett, F. W. (1982). Heterogeneous couples in heterosexual marriages: Gay men and straight women. *Journal of Marital and Family Therapy, 8*, 81–89.

Brick, P. (1991). Fostering positive sexuality. *Educational Leadership, 49*(1), 51–53.

Burr, C. (1993, August 2). Genes vs. hormones. *New York Times*, p. A11 (N), p. A15 (L).

Burr, C. (1993, March). Homosexuality and biology. *The Atlantic*, pp. 47–60.

Byne, W. (1994, May). The biological evidence challenged. *Scientific American, 270,* 50–55.

Cage, M. C. (1993, March 10). Openly gay students face harassment and physical assaults on some campuses. *Chronicle of Higher Education, 39*(27), A22.

Caywood, C. (1993, April). Reaching out to gay teens: Library materials that offer support to gay and lesbian teens can save lives. *School Library Journal,* 50.

Chan, C. S. (1989). Issues of identity development among Asian-American lesbians and gay men. *Journal of Counseling & Development, 68,* 16–20.

Clinton ends anti-gay security bias. (1995, August 5). *The Atlanta Journal/The Atlanta Constitution,* 8A.

Cohen, E. (1993, September 30). A house with no closets: Delta Lambda Phi is the first gay frat. *Rolling Stone,* p. 87.

Cranston, K. (1991). HIV education for gay, lesbian and bisexual youth: Personal risk, personal power, and the community of conscience. *Journal of Homosexuality, 22,* 247–259.

D'Augelli, A. R. (1992, September). Lesbian and gay male undergraduates' experiences of harassment and fear on campus. *Journal of Interpersonal Violence, 7*(3), 383.

Decter, M. (1993). Homosexuality and the schools. *Commentary, 95,* 19–25.

Dennis, D. I., & Harlow, R. E. (1986). Gay youth and the right to education. *Yale Law & Policy Review, 4*(2), 446–478.

Dorning, M. (1993, November 30). School's support groups helping gay teens to cope. *Chicago Tribune.*

Dougherty, J. W. (1990). *Effective programs for at-risk adolescents.* Fastback 308. Bloomington, IN: Phi Delta Kappa Educational Foundation.

Fefer, M. (1991, December 16). Gay in corporate America. *Fortune,* 42–54.

Fejes, F., & Petrich, K. (1993, December). Invisibility, homophobia and heterosexism: Lesbians, gays and the media. *Critical Studies in Mass Communication, 10*(4), 396.

Freund, K., Langevin, R., Cibiri, S., & Zajac, Y. (1973). Heterosexual aversion in homosexual males. *British Journal of Psychiatry, 122,* 163–169.

Friend, R. A. (1993, February). Undoing homophobia in schools. *Education Digest,* 62–68.

Gelman, D. (1993, November 8). Tune in and come out: Growing acceptance of gays and bisexuals in high schools. *Newsweek,* pp. 70–71.

Gibson, P. (1989). Gay male and lesbian youth suicide. In M. R. Feinleib (Ed.), *Report of the secretary's task force on youth suicide: Prevention and interventions in youth suicide* (Vol. 3, pp. 110–142). Washington, DC: U.S. Department of Health and Human Services.

Golombok, S., Spencer, A., & Rutter, M. (1983). Children in lesbian and single parent households: Psycho-sexual and psychiatric appraisal. *Journal of Child Psychology & Psychiatry, 24*(4), 551–572.

Gorski, R., Gordon, J., Shrine, J., & Southam, A. (1978). Evidence for a morphological sex difference within the medial pre-optic area of the rat brain. *Brain Research, 148,* 333–346.

Governor Weld offers aid to gay pupils: All schools in Massachusetts will be asked to promote more tolerant climate. (1993, July 4). *New York Times,* p. 11.

Governor's Commission on Gay and Lesbian Youth. (1993, February 25). *Making schools safe for gay and lesbian youth: Breaking the silence in schools and in families.* Publication #17296-60-500-2/93-C.R. Boston, MA: State House.

Green, J. (1993, June 13). Out and organized: As the national gay movement shies away from the subject of homosexuality among the young, some gay teen-agers are determined to open the subject up. *New York Times,* p. V1.

Green, R. (1978). Sexual identity of 37 children raised by homosexual or transsexual parents. *American Journal of Psychiatry, 135*(6), 692–697.

Griffin, P. (1992). From hiding out to coming out: Empowering lesbian and gay educators. *Journal of Homosexuality, 22,* 167–196.

Gross, J. (1991, February 11). New challenge of youth: Growing up in a gay home. *New York Times.*

Grossman, A. H. (1992). Inclusion not exclusion: Recreation service delivery to lesbian, gay and bisexual youth. *Journal of Physical Education, Recreation and Dance, 63*(4), 45–47.

Groth, A. N., & Birnbaum, H. J. (1978). Adult sexual orientation and attraction to underage children. *Archives of Sexual Behavior, 7*, 175–181.

Gurney, R. (1993, March). Looking for a safe haven: Helping students struggling with their sexual identity. *NEA Today, 11, 7*, 27.

Hamer, D., Hu, S., Magnuson, V., Hu, N., & Pattatucci, A. (1993, July 16). A linkage between DNA markers on the X chromosome and male sexual orientation. *Science, 261*, 321–327.

Harbeck, K. M. (1991). Gay and lesbian educators: Past history/future prospects. *Journal of Homosexuality, 22*, 121–139.

Harlan, H. (1992, April 5). Books help children of gay parents. *New York Times,* sec. 4A, p. ED8.

Harris, M. B., & Turner, P. H. (1986). Gay and lesbian parents. *Journal of Homosexuality, 12*, 101–113.

Heilbrun, A. B. (1976). The measurement of masculine and feminine sex role identities as independent dimensions. *Journal of Consulting Psychology, 44*, 143–190.

High school council passes a gay ban on leaders. (1993, May 16). *New York Times,* sec. 1, p. 17.

Hoeffer, B. (1981). Children's acquisition of sex-role behavior in lesbian-mother families. *American Journal of Orthopsychiatry, 51*(31), 536–543.

Hoffman, M. (1993, September). Teaching "Torch Song": Gay literature in the classroom ("Torch Song Trilogy" by Harvey Fierstein). *English Journal, 82*(5), 55–58.

Humm, A. J. (1982). Homosexuality: The new frontier in sexuality education. *Family Life Educator, 10*(3), 13–18.

Hunter, J. (1990). Violence against lesbian and gay male youths. *Journal of Interpersonal Violence, 5*(3), 295–300.

Hunter, J., & Schaecher, R. (1987). Stresses on lesbian and gay adolescents in schools. *Social Work in Education, 9,* 180–184.

Icard, L. (1986). Black gay men and conflicting social identities: Sexual orientation versus racial identity. *Journal of Social Work and Human Sexuality, 4,* 83–93.

Isay, R. A. (1985). On the analytic therapy of homosexual men. *Psychoanalytic Study of the Child, 40,* 235–254.

Isay, R. A. (1986). The development of sexual identity in homosexual men. *Psychoanalytic Study of the Child, 41,* 467–489.

Isay, R. A. (1987). Fathers and their homosexually inclined sons in childhood. *Psychoanalytic Study of the Child, 42,* 275–294.

Kirkpatrick, M., Smith, C., & Roy, R. (1981). Lesbian mothers and their children: A comparative study. *American Journal of Orthopsychiatry, 51*(3), 545–551.

Kournay, R. F. (1987). Suicide among homosexual adolescents. *Journal of Homosexuality, 13*(4), 111–117.

Krysiak, G. J. (1987, March). Needs of gay students for acceptance and support. *School Counselor, 34,* 304–307.

Lambda Legal Defense and Educational Fund Inc. (1993). New York: Author. (Available from the Lambda Legal Defense and Educational Fund Inc., 666 Broadway, New York, NY 10012)

LeVay, S. (1991, August 30). A difference in hypothalamic structure between heterosexual and homosexual men. *Science, 253,* 1034–1037.

LeVay, S., & Hamer, D. H. (1994, May). Evidence for a biological influence in male homosexuality. *Scientific American, 270,* 44–49.

Lewin, T. (1994, April 30). A killing in a small town becomes a chastening lesson in intolerance. *New York Times,* p. L8.

Lipkin, A. (1992, Fall). Project 10: Gay and lesbian students find acceptance in their school community. *Teaching Tolerance,* 25–27.

Mallon, G. (1992, November/December). Gay and no place to go: Assessing the needs of gay and lesbian adolescents in out-of-home care settings. *Child Welfare, 71*(6), 547.

Martin, A. D., & Hetrick, E. S. (1988). The stigmatization of the gay and lesbian adolescent. *Journal of Homosexuality, 15*(1/2), 163–183.

Martin, M. (1990). *Gay, lesbian, and heterosexual teachers: Acceptance of self, acceptance of others.* Unpublished report.

Masello, D. (1994, January 2). In my father's house. *New York Times Magazine,* p. 13.

McCord, D. M., & Herzog, H. A. (1991). What undergraduates want to know about homosexuality. *Teaching of Psychology, 18,* 243–244.

McFarland, W. P. (1993, September). A developmental approach to gay and lesbian youth. *Journal of Humanistic Education and Development, 32*(1), 17–29.

Mestel, R. (1994, January). X marks the spot. *Discover,* p. 71.

Mickens, E. (1994, April 9). Waging war on Wall Street. *The Advocate,* 40–45.

Miller, J. A., Mucklow, B. M., Jacobsen, R. B., & Bigner, J. J. (1980). Comparison of family relationships: Homosexual vs. heterosexual women. *Psychological Reports, 46,* 1127–1132.

National Education Association. (1988, July 7). Student sexual orientation. *National Education Association Resolution C-11.* Adopted by NEA in 1988 at NEA convention, New Orleans.

National Education Association. (1994). Teaching and counseling gay and lesbian students. *Human and civil rights action sheet.* Washington, DC: Author.

National Gay and Lesbian Task Force. (1993). *National Gay and Lesbian Task Force Policy Institute. Anti-gay/lesbian violence, victimization and defamation in 1992.* Washington, DC: Author.

New book series for gay teen-agers. (1992, November 24). *New York Times,* p. B3.

Newman, B. S., & Muzzonigro, P. G. (1993). The effects of traditional family values on the coming out process of gay male adolescents. *Adolescence, 28,* 213–226.

O'Connor, J. J. (1991, May 19). Gay's images: TV's mixed signals. *New York Times*, p. H1.

Ostling, R. N. (1992, March 16). Christians spar in Harvard yard. *Time*, p. 49.

Pagelow, M. (1980). Heterosexual and lesbian single mothers: A comparison of problems coping and solutions. *Journal of Homosexuality, 5*, 189–205.

Patterson, C. J. (1992). Children of lesbian and gay parents. *Child Development, 63*.

Petterson, N. (1984, April 30). Coming to terms with gay parents. *USA Today*, p. 30.

Pfeifer, J. K. (1986). *Teenage suicide: What can the schools do?* Fastback 234. Bloomington, IN: Phi Delta Kappa Educational Foundation.

Pillard, E., & Weinrich, J. (1986). Evidence of familial nature of male homosexuality. *Archives of General Psychiatry, 43*, 808–812.

Pool, R. (1993). Evidence for homosexuality gene. *Science, 261*, 291–292.

Remafedi, G. (1987). Homosexual youth: A challenge to contemporary society. *Journal of the American Medical Association, 258*, 222–225.

Remafedi, G. (1987). Male homosexuality: The adolescent's perspective. *Pediatrics, 79*, 326–330.

Remafedi, G. (1993, March). The impact of training on school professionals' knowledge, beliefs, and behaviors regarding HIV/AIDS and adolescent homosexuality. *Journal of School Health, 63*, 3.

Remafedi, G., Farrow, J. A., & Deisher, R. W. (1991, June). Risk factors for attempted suicide in gay and bisexual youth. *Pediatrics, 87*(6), 869–875.

Rimer, S. (1993, December 12). Massachusetts movement: Rights for gay students in public school. *New York Times*, p. E2.

Rofes, E. (1989). Opening up the classroom closet: Responding to the educational needs of gay and lesbian youth. *Harvard Educational Review, 59*, 443–453.

Rudolph, J. (1988, November). Counselors' attitudes toward homosexuality: A selective review of the literature. *Journal of Counseling & Development, 67*(3), 165–168.

Schaecher, R. (1989, Winter). Reducing homophobia among educators and students. *Independent School, 48,* 29–35.

School district allows gay students to meet. (1994, January 15). *New York Times,* p. 8.

Sears, J. T. (1987). Peering into the well of loneliness: The responsibility of educators to gay and lesbian youth. In A. Molnar (Ed.), *Social issues and education: Challenge and responsibility.* Alexandria, VA: Association for Supervision and Curriculum Development.

Sears, J. T. (1991). Educators, homosexuality and homosexual students: Are personal feelings related to professional beliefs? *Journal of Homosexuality, 22,* 29–79.

Sears, J. T. (1991, September). Helping students understand and accept sexual diversity. *Educational Leadership, 49*(1), 54–56.

Stewart, T. A. (1991, December 16). Gay in corporate America. *Fortune,* 42–55.

Stover, D. (1992, May). The at-risk students schools continue to ignore. *Educational Digest, 57, 9,* 36.

Tartagni, D. (1978). Counseling gays in a school setting. *School Counselor, 26,* 26–32.

Telljohann, S. K., & Price, J. H. (1993). A qualitative examination of adolescent homosexuals' life experiences: Ramifications for secondary school personnel. *Journal of Homosexuality, 26,* 41–56.

Treadway, L., & Yakum, J. (1992, September). Creating a safer school environment for lesbian and gay students. *Journal of School Health, 62, 7,* 352.

Tremble, B., Schneider, M., & Appathurai, C. (1989). Growing up gay or lesbian in a multicultural context. *Journal of Homosexuality, 17*(3/4), 253–267.

Troiden, R. R. (1989). The formation of homosexual identities. *Journal of Homosexuality, 17*(1–2), 43–73.

Turque, W., et al. (1992, September 14). Gays under fire. *Newsweek.*

Uribe, V., & Harbeck, K. M. (1991). Addressing the needs of lesbian, gay and bisexual youth. *Journal of Homosexuality, 22,* 9–28.

U.S. Department of Health and Human Services. (1989). *Report on the secretary's task force on youth suicide.* Washington, DC: Author.

Virginia school board prohibits anti-gay harassment by students. (1992, July 27). *New York Times*, p. A7.

Wagner, G., Serafini, J., Rabin, J., Remien, R., & Williams, J. (1994). Integration of one's religion and homosexuality: A weapon against internalized homophobia? *Journal of Homosexuality, 26*(4), 91–110.

Walling, D. R. (1993). Gay teens at risk. *Fastback series of Phi Delta Kappa Educational Foundation* (p. 371). Bloomington, IN: Phi Delta Kappa Educational Foundation.

Weiner, H. (1994, December 28). More companies adding benefits for partners of gays and lesbians. *Miami Herald*, 8C.

Will all the homophobes please stand up? (1994, June 20). *New York*, 40–45.

Williams, R. F. (1993, Spring). Gays and lesbian teenagers: A reading ladder for students, media specialists and parents. *ALAN Review, 20*(3), 12–17.

Willis, S. (1991, March). Teaching gay students. *ASCD Update, 33*, 3.

Wilson, P. M. (1986). Black culture and sexuality. *Journal of Social Work and Human Sexuality, 4*(3), 29–46.

Winerip, M. (1994, February 23). A high school club for gay students has gained a foothold, though not everyone may feel secure. *New York Times*, p. B7.

Zera, D. (1992, Winter). Coming of age in a heterosexist world: The development of gay and lesbian adolescents. *Adolescence, 27*, 108, 849–854.

BROCHURES, HANDBOOKS, RESOURCE GUIDES, AND CURRICULUM MATERIALS

Affording Equal Opportunity to Gay and Lesbian Students through Teaching and Counseling. National Education Association, 1201 Sixteenth Street, N.W., Washington, DC 20036; (202) 822-7730.

Equity Education and Safer Schools, Colleges and Universities. Association for Supervision and Curriculum Development, P.O. Box 27527, Oakland, CA 94602; (510) 642-7329.

Family Life Education Curriculum. Fairfax County Public Schools, Department for Secondary Instruction, 10700 Page Avenue, Fairfax, VA 22030; (703) 246-2502.

"Gay Male and Lesbian Youth Suicide." *Report of the Secretary's Task Force on Youth Suicide.* Vol. 3. Prevention and Interventions in Youth Suicide. U.S. Department of Health and Human Services, Public Health Service, Alcohol, Drug Abuse and Mental Health Administration Publication No. (ADM) 89-1623. Superintendent of Documents, U.S. Government Printing Office, Washington, DC 20401; (202) 512-1800.

"The Gay Teenager." *The High School Journal,* vol. 77, nos. 1-2. University of North Carolina Press, Box 2288, Chapel Hill, NC 27515-2288; (919) 966-3561; fax (919) 966-3829.

Homophobia: Discrimination Based on Sexual Orientation. Gay and Lesbian Alliance Against Defamation (GLAAD), 1875 Connecticut Avenue, N.W., #640, Washington, DC 20009; (202) 986-1360; fax (202) 667-0902; e-mail: ⟨glaad@glaad.org⟩; ⟨http://www.glaad.org⟩.

Human Sexuality Course material. c/o Barbara Blinick, Support Services for Gay and Lesbian Youth, San Francisco United School District, 1512 Golden Gate Avenue, San Francisco, CA 94115; (415) 749-3400.

Massachusetts Department of Education Safe Schools Workshop. Massachusetts Department of Education, Learning Support Services, 350 Main Street, Malden, MA 02148; (617) 388-3300.

One Out of Ten Students: A Resource Directory for Teachers, Guidance Counselors, Parents, and School-Based Adolescent-Care Providers. The Personal Fund, P.O. Box 1431, New Brunswick, NJ 08903; (908) 469-9135.

Project for the Study of Gay and Lesbian Issues in Schools. Dr. Arthur Lipkin, Harvard Graduate School of Education, 210 Longfellow Hall, Cambridge, MA 02138; (617) 491-5301.

Sexuality and the Curriculum. James T. Sears, Teachers College Press, 1234 Amsterdam Avenue, New York, NY 10027; (212) 678-3929.

Struggle for Equality: The Lesbian and Gay Community. PACE, 115 W. 28th Street, #3-R, New York, NY 10001; (212) 643-8490.

AUDIOTAPES

Accepting Your Gay or Lesbian Child: Parents Share Their Stories. Sounds True, 735 Walnut Street, Boulder, CO 80302.

Barne, H. (1995). *Reaching Out to and Educating Community/Corporate Leaders.* Parents, Families and Friends of Lesbians and Gays Convention. National Recording Services, Inc., 8500 N. Stemmons, Suite 3060, Dallas, TX 75247; (214) 638-8273; fax (214) 638-0954.

Gore, S. (1995). *Opening Corporate America to P-FLAG.* Parents, Families and Friends of Lesbians and Gays Convention. National Recording Services, Inc., 8500 N. Stemmons, Suite 3060, Dallas, TX 75247; (214) 638-8273; fax (214) 638-0954.

Kunreuther, F. (1995). *The Challenges and Opportunities in 1996 for Gay, Lesbian, Bisexual and Transgendered Youth.* Parents, Families and Friends of Lesbians and Gays Convention. National Recording Services, Inc., 8500 N. Stemmons, Suite 3060, Dallas, TX 75247; (214) 638-8273; fax (214) 638-0954.

McNaught, B. (1995). *Gays and Lesbians in the Workplace Environment.* Parents, Families and Friends of Lesbians and Gays Convention. National Recording Services, Inc., 8500 N. Stemmons, Suite 3060, Dallas, TX 75247; (214) 638-8273; fax (214) 638-0954.

O'Mara, M. (1995). *Teens Tell Their Own Stories.* Parents, Families and Friends of Lesbians and Gays Convention. National Recording Services, Inc., 8500 N. Stemmons, Suite 3060, Dallas, TX 75247; (214) 638-8273; fax (214) 638-0954.

Wilson, J., & Woog, D. (1995). *So Just What Does a School Board Do?* Parents, Families and Friends of Lesbians and Gays Convention. National Recording Services, Inc., 8500 N. Stemmons, Suite 3060, Dallas, TX 75247; (214) 638-8273; fax (214) 638-0954.

VIDEOTAPES

A Little Respect. (25 minutes). Rutgers State University, Department of Health Education, University Heights, 299 University Avenue, Newark, NJ 07102; (201) 648-1236.

Before Stonewall: The Making of a Gay and Lesbian Community. (1984; 87 minutes). This video portrays the history of homosexual experience in America from the 1920s to recent times. It traces the social, political, and cultural development of the lesbian and gay community and a period of remarkable social change in America. The Cinema Guild, 1697 Broadway, Suite 506, New York, NY 10019-5904; (212) 246-5522; fax (212) 246-5525; orders only (800) 723-5522. Also available in many public library video collections.

Both of My Moms' Names Are Judy. (10 minutes). The video presents a racially diverse group of children (ages 7–10) talking about the love they feel for their families, how teasing and classroom silence about lesbians and gay men affects them, and the changes they would like to see. (Intended audience: elementary educators.) Lesbian and Gay Parents Association, GLPCI, Box 43206, Montclair, NJ 07043; (202) 583-8029.

Gay Issues in the Workplace: Gay, Lesbian and Bisexual Employees Speak for Themselves with Brian McNaught. (1993; 25 minutes). TRB Productions, PO Box 2362, Boston, MA 02107; (617) 236-7800.

Gay Youth. (40 minutes). Pam Walton, Wolfe Video, P.O. Box 64, New Almaden, CA 95042; (408) 268-6782.

Homosexuality: The Adolescent's Perspective. (1987; 30 minutes). Produced by Gary Remafedi, M.D., M.P.H. Six teenagers describe their lives to viewers. University of Minnesota, Media Distribution, Box 734 Mayo, 420 Delaware Street, S.E., Minneapolis, MN 55455; (612) 624-7906.

Not All Parents Are Straight. (1986; 58 minutes). This video examines the dynamics of parent–child relationships within several different households where children are being raised by gay and lesbian parents. The Cinema Guild, 1697 Broadway, Suite 506, New York, NY 10019-5904; (212) 246-5522; fax (212) 246-5525; orders only (800) 723-5522.

On Being Gay: A Conversation with Brian McNaught. (80 minutes). TRB Productions, P.O. Box 2362, Boston, MA 02107; (617) 236-7800.

Pink Triangles: A Study of Prejudice Against Lesbians and Gay Men. (35 minutes). An award-winning documentary on homophobia. Cambridge Documentary Films, Inc., P.O. Box 385, Cambridge, MA 02139; (617) 354-3677 and (617) 492-7653.

Running Gay. (1991; 20 minutes). This video examines the participation of lesbians and gay men in sports and highlights the third annual International Gay

Games held in Vancouver in August 1990, in which 7,300 athletes participated. The Cinema Guild, 1697 Broadway, Suite 506, New York, NY 10019-5904; (212) 246-5522; fax (212) 246-5525; orders only (800) 723-5522.

Sexual Orientation: Reading Between the Labels. (1991; 30 minutes). Personal accounts from lesbian and gay teenagers are interspersed with input from professional workers and parents of gay and lesbian teenagers. NEWIST/CESA #7 Telecommunications IS 1110, University of Wisconsin, Green Bay, WI 54311; (414) 465-2599.

Sticks, Stones, and Stereotypes (Palos, Piedras, y Estereotipos). (20 minutes; Spanish and English versions). The Equity Institute, Tucker-Taft Building, 48 N. Pleasant Street, Amherst, MA 01002; (413) 256-0271.

21st Century News Human Rights Video Series. This series is being used by schools and counselors to increase awareness, promote discussion, and help eradicate homophobia in our society. The following videotapes are available from 21st Century News, Inc., P.O. Box 42286, Tucson, AZ 85733; (602) 577-1137.

> *Another Side of the Closet.* (30 minutes). Three former spouses of gay men discuss the process of when their husbands acknowledged their homosexuality. Their honest sharing provides insight and hope for others in similar situations.
> *Be True to Yourself.* (28 minutes). Authors and human rights activists Bob and Rod Jackson-Paris talk with ten teenagers about growing up gay, self-esteem, and the courage to be true to yourself.
> *Families Come Out.* (30 minutes). This program offers insight and support to the one in four families with a gay, lesbian, or bisexual person in the immediate family. Families share their experiences in dealing with a son or daughter, sister, brother, or parent coming out of the closet.
> *Reunion: One Family Overcomes Religious Homophobia.* (30 minutes). This video features Dr. Carter Heyward, a lesbian ordained Episcopal priest, author, and professor of theology. Dr. Heyward and her family discuss their process of reconciling religious beliefs about homosexuality with their love for each other.
> *Teens Speak Out.* (45 minutes). A young lesbian and two gay men discuss their lives and their process of coming out. Two black participants discuss what it is like to be part of a double minority.

What If I'm Gay?: A Search for Understanding. (1988; 29- and 47-minute versions). Coronet/MTI Film and Video, 108 Wilmot Road, Deerfield, IL 60015; (800) 621-2131.

Who's Afraid of Project 10? (1990; 23 minutes). A debate over counseling services for gay and lesbian youth in the Los Angeles public schools. Contact Scott Greene for availability: (213) 656-7327.

ORGANIZATIONS

American Civil Liberties Union (ACLU), National Gay & Lesbian Rights Project, 132 West 43rd Street, New York, NY 10036; (212) 944-9800 (ext. 545); ⟨http://www.aclu.org/action/mailist.html⟩ or ⟨http://www.aclu.org/issues/gay/irgl.html⟩. ("Domestic Partnership Information Packet," 1992)

American Federation of Teachers, Gay and Lesbian Caucus, P.O. Box 19856, Cincinnati, OH; (513) 242-2491; ⟨http://www.aft.org:80/aboutaft/main.htm⟩.

American Library Association, Gay & Lesbian Task Force, 50 E. Huron Street, Chicago, IL 60611; (312) 280-4294; fax (312) 280-3256; ⟨http://www. ala.org:80/Architect/AT-webdataquery.html⟩ or ⟨http://www.ala.org:80/index. html⟩.

American Psychiatric Association, Division of Minority/National Affairs, 1400 K Street, N.W., Washington, DC 20005; (202) 682-6097; ⟨http://www.thebody. com:80/apa/apdpage.html⟩.

American Psychological Association, Committee on Lesbian & Gay Concerns, 1200 17th Street, N.W., Washington, DC 20036; (202) 955-7649; ⟨http://www. apa.org:80/⟩.

American School Counselor Association, 5999 Stevenson Avenue, Alexandria, VA 22304; (703) 823-9800; ⟨http://www.edge.net:80/asca/aboutasca.html⟩.

Association for Supervision and Curriculum Development, 1250 N. Pitt Street, Alexandria, VA 22314; (703) 549-9110; ⟨http://www.ascd.org:80/⟩.

Bridges Project of American Friends Service Committee, National Coalition for Youth and Sexual Orientation, 1501 Cherry Street, Philadelphia, PA 19102; (215) 741-7000.

Center for Lesbian and Gay Studies, CUNY Graduate Center (City University of New York), 33 West 42nd Street, New York, NY 10036; (212) 642-2924; fax (212) 642-2642. Promotes gay and lesbian studies at the university level; publishes a directory of lesbian and gay scholars.

Children of Lesbians and Gays Everywhere (COLAGE), 2300 Market Street, Box 165, San Francisco, CA 94114; (415) 861-5437; fax (415) 255-8345; e-mail: ⟨KidsOfGays@aol.com⟩.

Contact for a directory of national and international member chapters and legal resources for lesbians and gay parents.

Conference for Catholic Lesbians, P.O. Box 436, Planetarium Station, New York, NY 10024; (813) 822-5030.

Friends of Project 10, Inc., 7850 Melrose Avenue, Los Angeles, CA 90046; (213) 651-5200; ⟨http://www.lausd.kld.ca.us.⟩.

Gay & Lesbian Association of the U.S. Small Business Association, Don Kraft, 409 3rd Street, S.W., Washington, DC 20416; (202) 205-6605; ⟨http://www.sheppinc.com:80/us.htm⟩.

Gay and Lesbian Alliance Against Defamation (GLAAD), P.O. Box 741346, Los Angeles, CA 90004; (213) 931-9429.

Gay and Lesbian Parents Coalition International (GLPCI network), P.O. Box 50360, Washington, DC 20091; (202) 583-8029; fax (201) 783-6204; e-mail: ⟨GLPCIN@ix.netcom.com⟩; ⟨http://ericps.ed.uiuc.edu:80/npin/parlink.html⟩.

Gay, Lesbian and Straight Teachers Network (GLSTN), P.O. Box 390526, Cambridge, MA 02139.

Gay and Lesbian Victory Fund, 1012 14th Street, NW (Suite 707), Washington, DC 20005; (202) VICTORY; e-mail: ⟨VictoryF.@aol.com⟩. Political network supporting openly gay and lesbian candidates for public office.

Hetrick-Martin Institute, 2 Astor Place, New York, NY 10003; (212) 674-2400; fax (212) 674-8650; e-mail: ⟨hmi@hmi.org⟩; ⟨http://soho.ios.com: 80~msmigels/glcd/h-milk.html⟩. Informs and educates public and youth services about the needs of gay and lesbian youth.

Lesbian, Bisexual, and Gay United Employees at AT&T, 11900 Pecos Street, #30H-078, Denver, CO 80234-2703; (303) 538-4430; fax (303) 538-3564. Information clearinghouse, educational programs, and support groups; created for employees and retirees of AT&T and all its subsidiaries; 25 state groups.

Lesbian, Gay and Bisexual Issues in Education: A Network of the Association of Supervision and Curriculum Development, P.O. Box 27527, Oakland, CA 94602; (510) 642-7329.

National Association of Social Workers, 7981 Eastern Avenue, Silver Springs, MD 20910; (301) 565-0333; ⟨http://www.electriciti.com:80/~sdrl/nasw.html⟩.

National Education Association (NEA), Gay and Lesbian Caucus, P.O. Box 3559, York, PA 17402-0559; (717) 840-0903; ⟨http://query.webrawler.com:80/select/ed.75.html⟩.

National Education Association (NEA), Human and Civil Rights, 1201 Sixteenth Street, N.W., Washington, DC 20036; (202) 822-7700.

National Gay and Lesbian Task Force Policy Institute, 1734 Fourteenth Street, N.W., Washington, DC 20009-4309; (202) 332-6483.

National Latino: A Lesbian and Gay Organization, Box 44483, Washington, DC 20026.

Out At work (or Not), Jason Cohen, P.O. Box 359, Chicago, IL 606090-0359; (312) 794-5218.

P-FLAG [Parents, Families and Friends of Lesbians and Gays (national network)], 1101 14th Street, N.W., Suite 1030, Washington, DC 20005; (202) 638-4200; e-mail: ⟨PFLAGNTL@aol.com⟩; ⟨http://www.nz.qrd.org:80/qrd/orgs/PFLAG/misc/letters.to.networks⟩. ("Lesbigay Workplace Issues Resource Directory," 1994)

SAGE (Seniors Active in a Gay Environment), 208 West 13th Street, New York, NY 10011; (212) 741-2247; fax (212) 366-1947. Intergenerational social service organization for gay and lesbian senior citizens.

Straight Spouse Support Network, 8215 Terrace Drive, El Cerrito, CA 94530; (510) 525-0200.

World Congress of Gays/Lesbians Jewish Organization, Box 3345, New York, NY 10008-3345; ⟨http://www.qrd.org:80/qrd/www/orgs/sssn/home.htm⟩.

HOTLINES

Deaf Community Aids Hotline (TTY/TDD), 800-243-7889 (Monday through Friday).

IYG Gay/Lesbian/Bisexual Youth Hotline, 800-347-8336 (Thursday through Sunday). Peer counseling and information for youth under 21 years of age.

Linea National de SIDA (Spanish AIDS Hotline), 800-344-7432 (daily).

National AIDS Hotline, 800-342-AIDS (24-hour service), 800-AIDS-TTY (hearing impaired).

National Gay & Lesbian Crisis Line, 800-767-4297. Crisis intervention, information, and referral.

National Runaway Switchboard, 800-621-4000 (7 days a week, 24 hours). Hotline for runaway/homeless youth and their families.

U.S. Justice Department National Hate Crime Reporting Number, 800-347-HATE.

EVALUATION OF THE WORKSHOP

Workshop evaluations provide valuable information for facilitators in terms of planning for subsequent workshops. There are two different evaluation forms (A and B) in this section, each of which addresses a variety of topics and provides feedback related to workshop content, facilitators' skills, suggestions for subsequent workshops, and how participants were individually affected by the workshop. The choice of which form to use is left to the facilitators.

Activity 13.1
EVALUATION OF THE WORKSHOP

Objective: To obtain participants' feedback concerning the workshop
Estimated Time: 15 to 20 minutes
Materials Needed: Workshop Evaluation: Form A or Form B

Directions for Facilitators

1. Explain the importance of participants' feedback as it relates to:
    a. the appropriateness of the workshop content,
    b. the effectiveness of the facilitators,
    c. application of the content in the participants' workplace/educational settings, and
    d. changes in individual participants' thinking and perceptions concerning the various topics dealt with through the workshop activities.
2. Distribute the chosen evaluation form (one for each participant) and participants to complete the form in approximately 15 minutes.
3. Collect completed forms.

FORM A

Workshop Title _____

Location _____ Date(s)_____

Trainers' Names_____

1. Did the workshop cover content you need to help you in your current position?
   Yes_____ No_____
   If not, what should have been included? _____

   _____

   _____

   _____

2. Do you think the content and training aids were
   a. adequate for use during the workshop?
   Yes_____ No_____
   If not, what changes would you suggest? _____

   _____

   _____

   _____

   b. adequate for reference and use in your current position?
   Yes_____ No_____
   If not, what changes would you suggest? _____

   _____

   _____

   _____

3. Were the training methods adequate?
   Yes_____ No_____
   If not, what changes would you suggest? _____

   _____

   _____

   _____

4. Please rate the trainers' facilitation skills. (Circle the appropriate numbers.)

	Low			High	
a. Questioning skills	1	2	3	4	5
b. Responding skills	1	2	3	4	5
c. Paying attention to the learners	1	2	3	4	5
d. Listening skills	1	2	3	4	5

5. Which ONE exercise from the workshop will be most useful to you in your current position?_____

_____

_____

6. Any other comments? (Use the back of this page, if necessary.) _____

_____

_____

_____

(Thank you for completing this evaluation.)

Handout Form A.   Permission is granted to photocopy for classroom use.

FORM B

Workshop Title _____
Location _____ Date(s)_____
Trainers' Names_____

Directions: Please rate the facilitators by placing an "X" in the appropriate column:

Facilitators	Excellent	Good	Fair	Poor
Overall presentation	___	___	___	___
Accomplishment of workshop goals	___	___	___	___
Preparation	___	___	___	___
Organizational skills	___	___	___	___
Skills in promoting discussion	___	___	___	___
Knowledge of content	___	___	___	___

Please complete the following:

1.   Before this workshop, I believed:_____
_____
_____
_____

2.   As a result of the workshop, now I believe:_____
_____
_____
_____

3.   What would you recommend to improve the workshop? _____
_____
_____
_____

4. Two things I learned about myself as a result of the workshop are:

    a. _____
    _____
    _____
    _____

    b. _____
    _____
    _____
    _____

5. What additional comments or observations would you like to make? _____
    _____
    _____
    _____
    _____
    _____
    _____

(Thank you for completing this evaluation.)

Handout Form B.   Permission is granted to photocopy for classroom use.

INDEX

ABOUT THE AUTHORS

Hilda F. Besner, Ph.D., is a licensed clinical psychologist in private practice, with 22 years of experience working with gay and lesbian clients and their families. Her publications encompass books and articles on various topics, including marriage and family problems, biofeedback, and the emotional impact and aftereffects of Hurricane Andrew. She is co-author of *Gay and Lesbian Students: Understanding Their Needs* (1995, Taylor & Francis). Dr. Besner has been honored for her professional and community leadership and service through the following awards: "Outstanding Contribution by a Psychologist for Community Services Award," sponsored by the Florida Psychological Association; "Woman of the Year Award," sponsored by the organization of National Business and Professional Women; and the "Outstanding Young Career Woman Award," also sponsored by the organization of National Business and Professional Women.

Charlotte Spungin, Ed.S., is an education consultant with 29 years of public school classroom experience teaching psychology at the 12-grade level. Having extensive experience in curriculum writing and staff development, she is co-author of the national curriculum guide for the PBS television series "Creativity with Bill Moyers." She is co-author of a textbook, *Psychology: Understanding Ourselves and Others*, and of the book *Gay & Lesbian Students: Understanding Their Needs*. The recipient of the National Science Foundation and Fulbright Scholar awards, Ms. Spungin also has received many professional and community awards, including the prestigious Miami Herald "Spirit of Excellence" award. She is currently professionally active in training teachers.